*******CHORDS AND SCALES FOR THE GUITAR******

A REMARKABLE AND MODERN BOOK FOR ALL STYLES OF PLAYING

———————————————————————————— BY ARTHUR BAYAS

CONTENTS

COPYRIGHT 1979 BY LEWIS MUSIC PUBLISHING CO.

Lewis Publications, 133 Industrial Avenue, Hasbrouck Heights, NJ 07604

HOW TO TUNE YOUR GUITAR

The six strings of your guitar are the same pitch as the six notes shown on the piano in the following illustration:

(With The Piano)

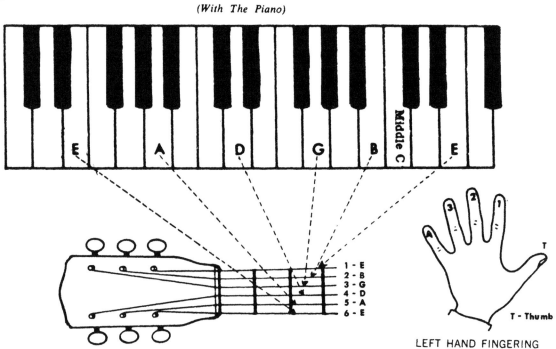

LEFT HAND FINGERING

ANOTHER WAY OF TUNING YOUR GUITAR

Tune the 6th string to E on the piano. If no piano is available, approximate E as best you can and proceed as follows:

Press 5th fret of 6th string to get pitch of 5th string (A).
Press 5th fret of 5th string to get pitch of 4th string (D).
Press 5th fret of 4th string to get pitch of 3rd string (G).
Press 4th fret of 3rd string to get pitch of 2nd string (B).
Press 5th fret of 2nd string to get pitch of 1st string (E).

It is recommended that a guitar pitch pipe be used when a piano is not available. They are available at your music store.

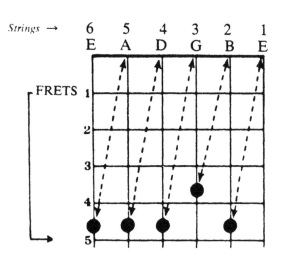

The name of each chord, called the chord SYMBOL, is shown over each diagram. The letter in the symbol (frequently with a sharp or flat next to it) shows the ROOT of the chord which is the note upon which the chord is constructed. If the symbol consists only of the name of the root, a MAJOR chord is indicated. This is a chord of a specific type, the construction of which will be explained later.

Additional information in the form of abbreviations may also appear. Here are some of them, with their meanings.

m (or mi.) shows a type of chord called a MINOR chord.
7 shows a DOMINANT SEVENTH chord.
dim. (or dim. 7, or o, or —) shows a DIMINISHED SEVENTH chord.
+ (or aug.) shows an AUGMENTED FIFTH chord.
m7 shows a MINOR SEVENTH chord.

Next is shown the diagram for a specific chord, and how to interpret it.

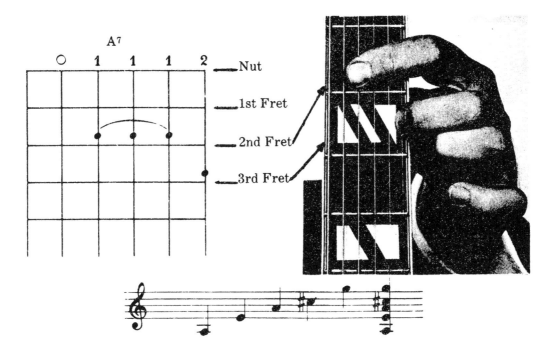

Above, the chord symbol shows that the note A is the chord root. The 7 shows that it is a dominant seventh chord (frequently called simply a SEVENTH chord).

Reading from left to right, you see that the sixth string has no information above it, therefore it will not be used in playing the chord. The 5th string is played open, and by looking at the music under it you see that it produces the note A. The 4th, 3rd, and 2nd strings are pressed by the 1st finger at the 2nd fret (BARRE). Actually, the 1st finger also presses the 1st string at the 2nd fret, but this will not affect the note played on the 1st string, since it is fingered at the 3rd fret by the 2nd finger. The notes sounded on the 4th, 3rd, 2nd, and 1st strings are shown below them in the music, and finally the music shows the complete chord.

Diagrams for the chords in the first series are shown on the following pages. These are for a straight chord accompaniment, and may be played either with a pick, or finger style. The six types of chords in this series are sufficient for accompanying most folk style songs and many popular type songs with a relatively simple harmonization.

A convenient way to become proficient in playing these chords is to play each line of chords from left to right, strumming each chord several times.

FIRST SERIES OF CHORDS

MAJOR CHORDS

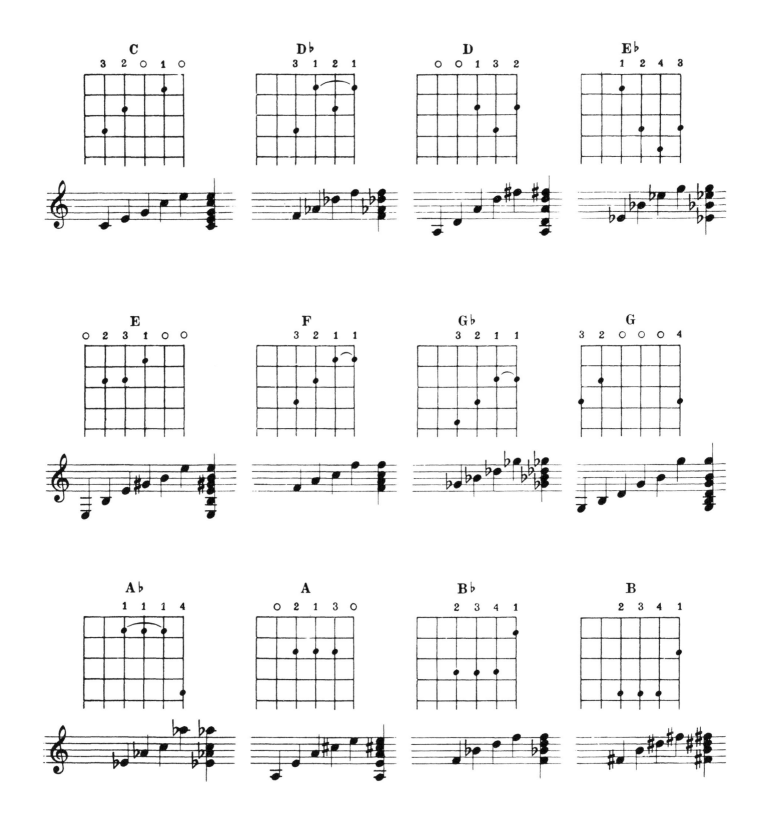

MINOR CHORDS

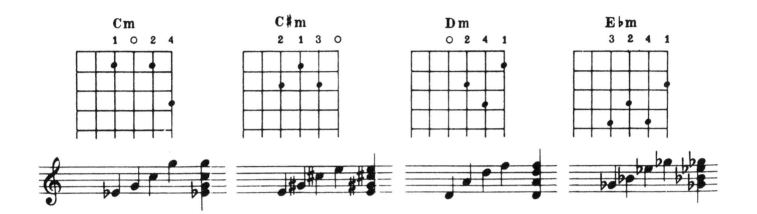

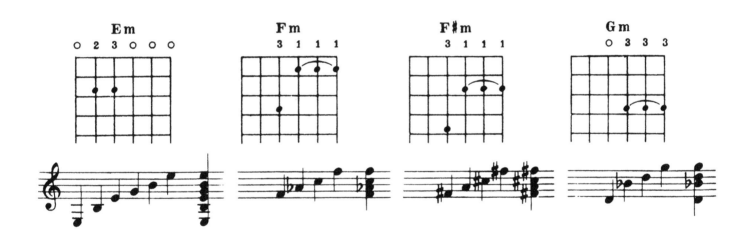

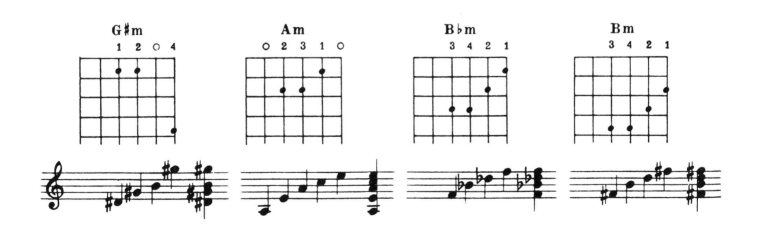

6

DOMINANT SEVENTH CHORDS

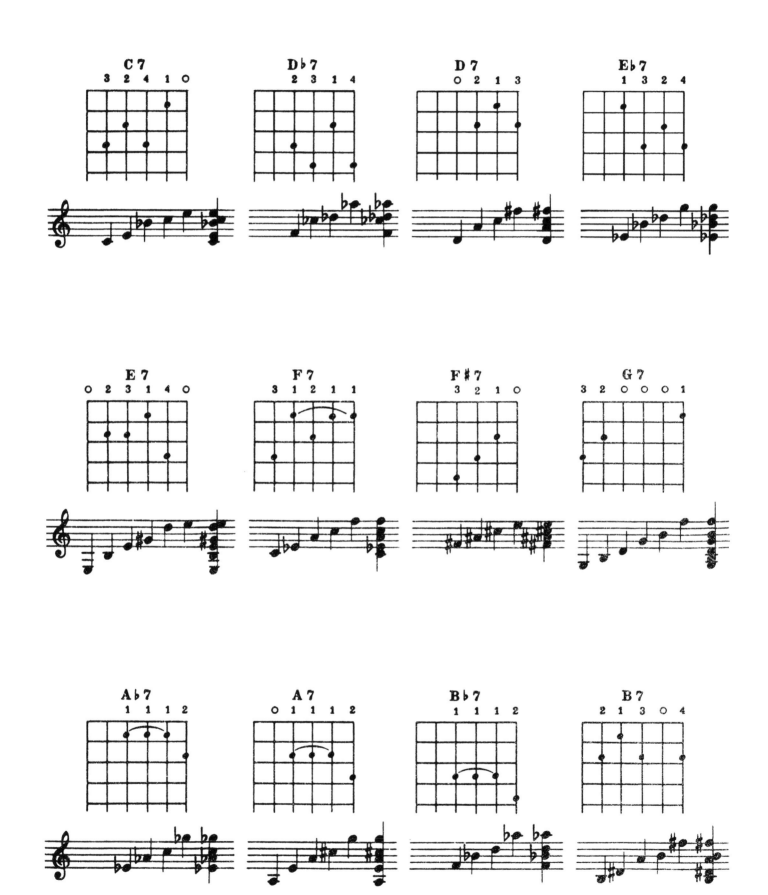

DIMINISHED SEVENTH CHORDS

You need to learn only three diminished seventh (also known simply as DIMINISHED) chords, because each of the diagrams shown can be used for four different chord symbols.

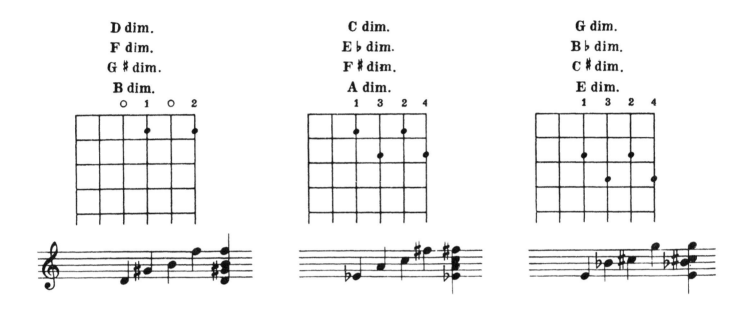

AUGMENTED FIFTH CHORDS

You need to learn only four augmented fifth (also known simply as AUGMENTED) chords, because each of the diagrams shown can be used for three different chord symbols.

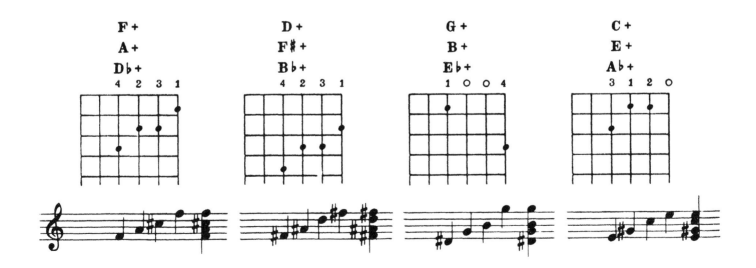

8

MINOR SEVENTH CHORDS

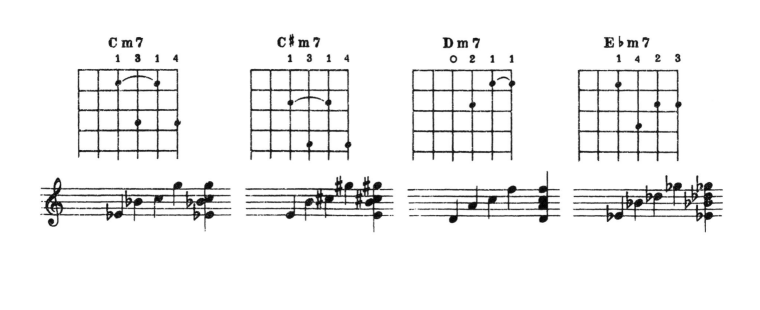

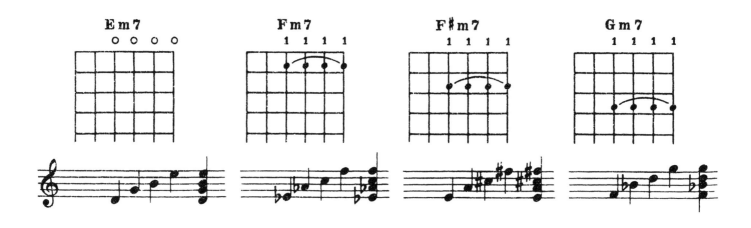

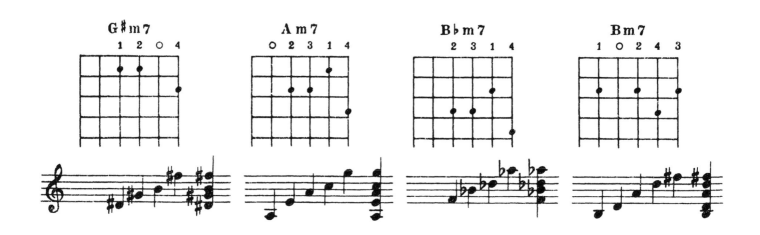

SECOND SERIES OF CHORDS

The formations shown in the second series are for playing bass notes (individual low notes) alternating with chords. A bass note that is fingered is shown by a black diamond within the diagram: a bass note played on an open string is shown by a white diamond over the string. The chords used to alternate with the bass notes consist of notes shown on the diagrams other than by diamonds. On a diagram showing both bass notes played by the same finger, unless a curved line appears the finger moves from one string to the other. Notice that some chords have only one bass note indicated.

MAJOR CHORDS

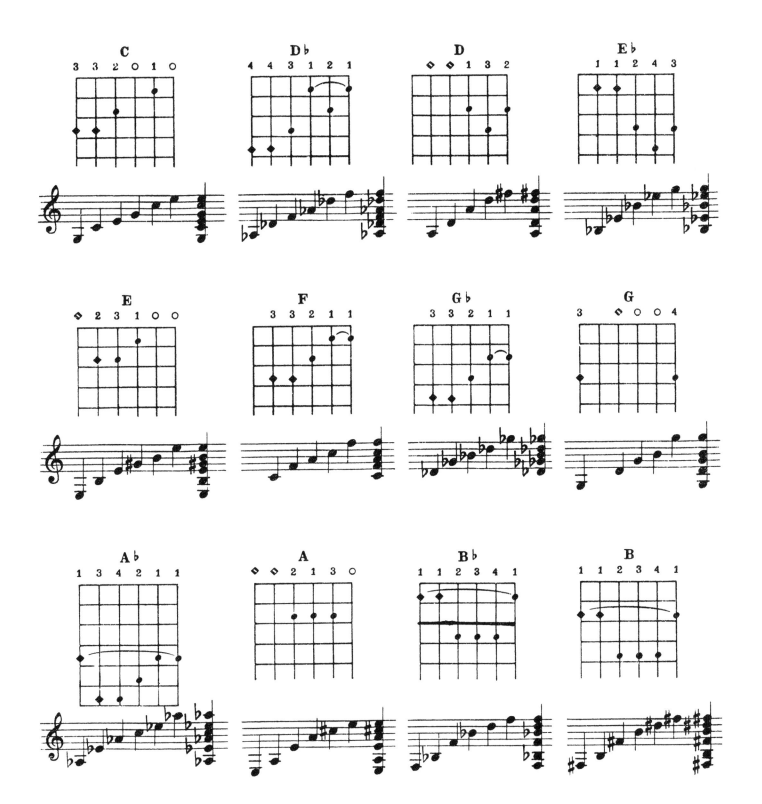

MINOR CHORDS

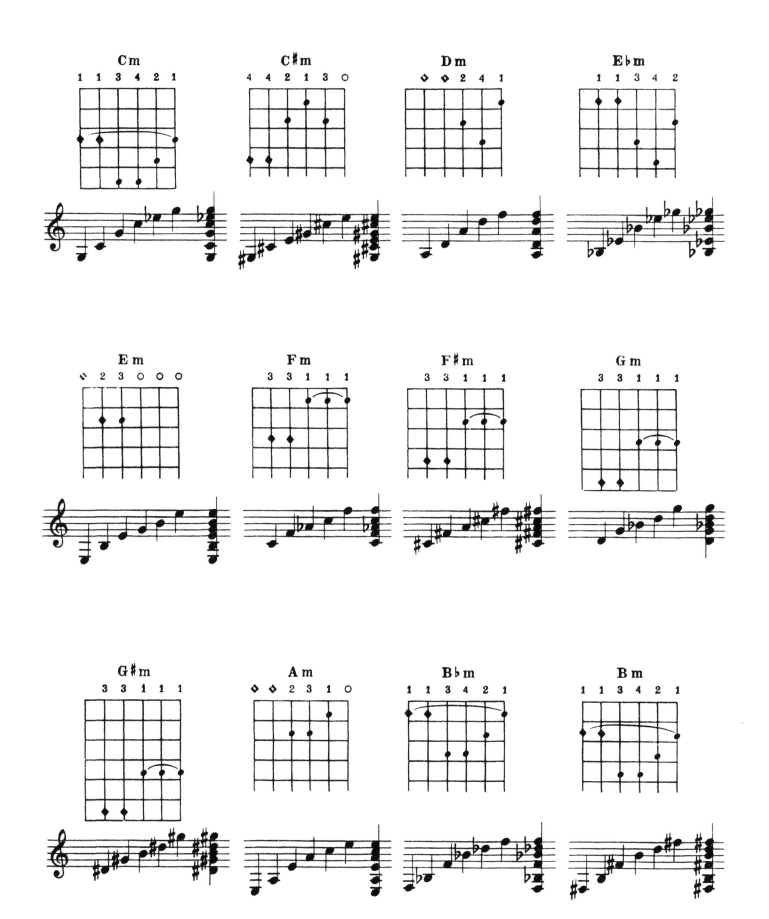

DOMINANT SEVENTH CHORDS

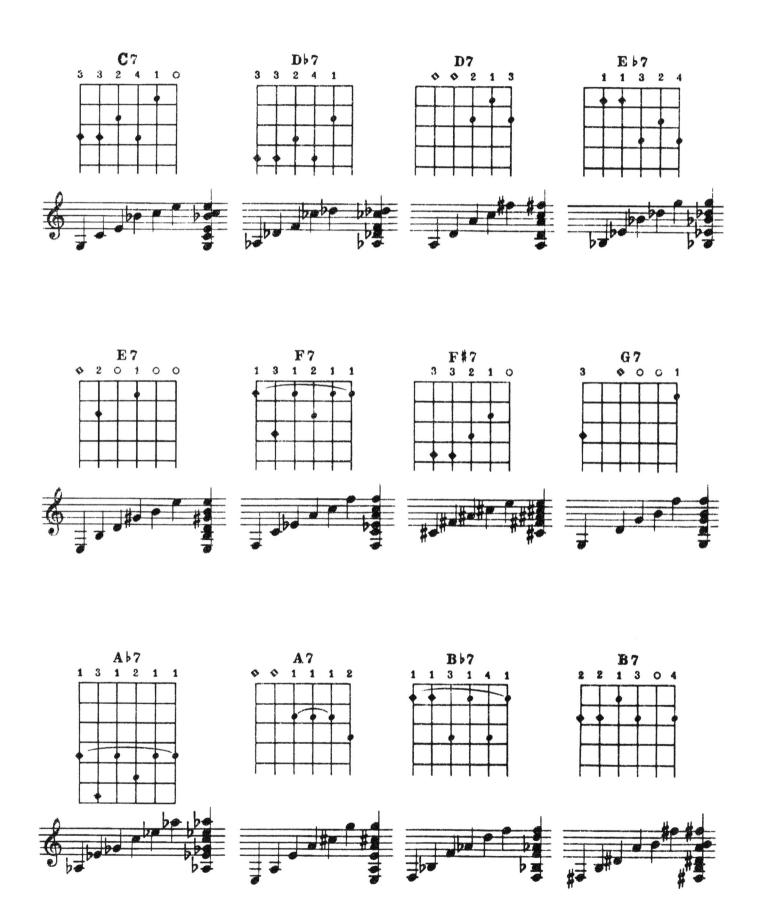

DIMINISHED SEVENTH CHORDS

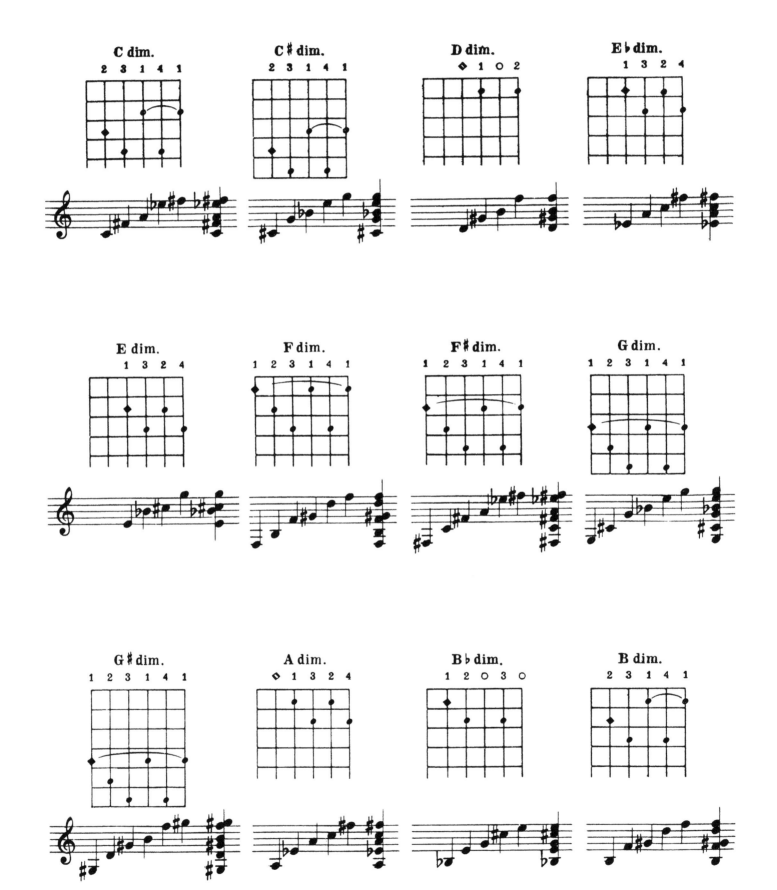

AUGMENTED FIFTH CHORDS

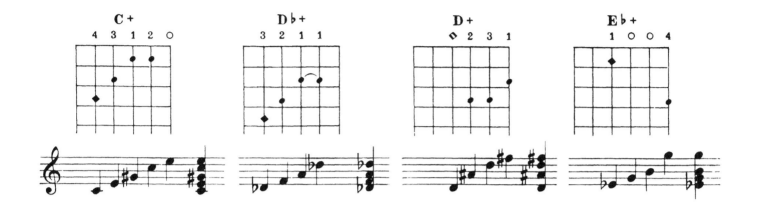

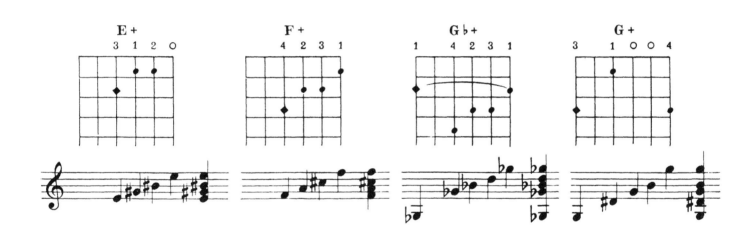

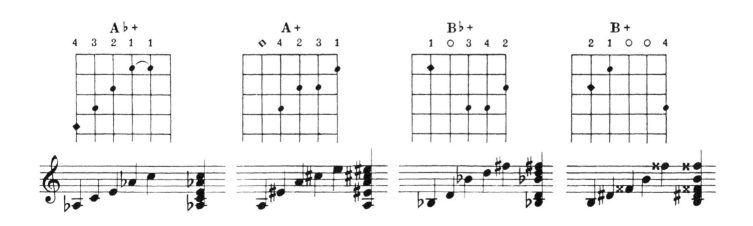

MINOR SEVENTH CHORDS

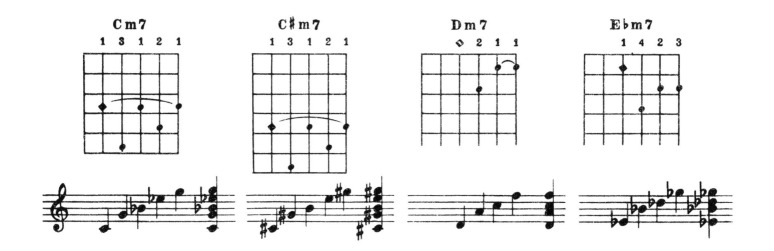

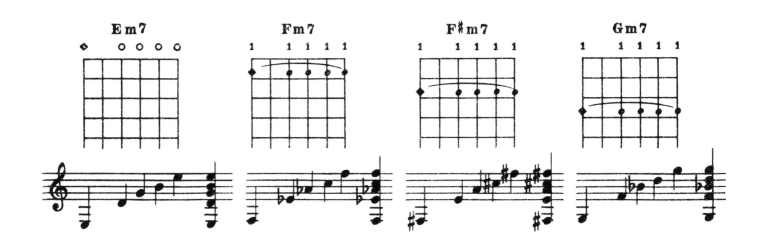

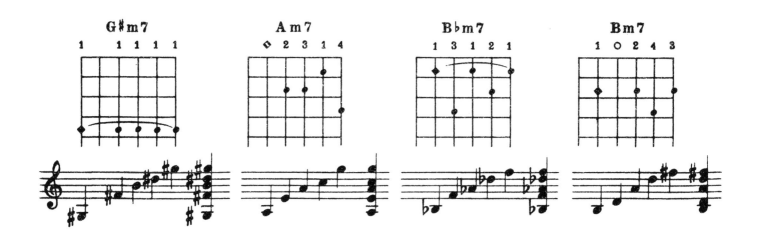

CHORD CONSTRUCTION EXPLAINED

A knowledge of INTERVALS is essential to the understanding of chord construction. An interval is the distance, or difference in pitch, between the sounds produced by playing two notes placed one on top of the other on the staff. Intervals are considered to be made up of whole steps and half steps. On the guitar, to move from one tone to another a whole step higher, you move to the right (up the fingerboard) two frets. One fret gives a half step.

You may identify any interval by carefully comparing it with those given in the table below, in which the name of the interval and the number of whole and half steps in each are shown above the sample.

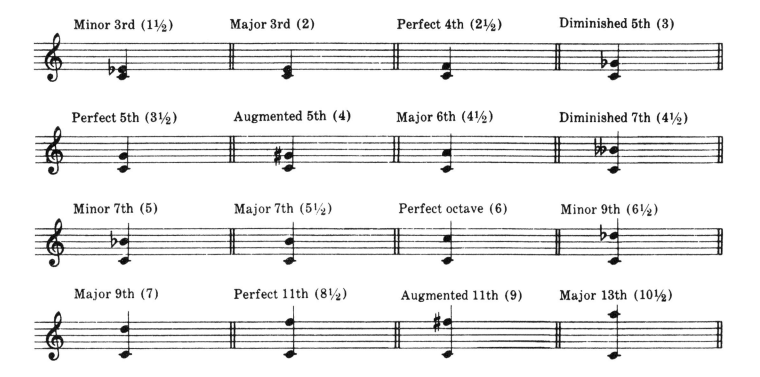

Next are shown chords you have already played, and how they are constructed. Each chord is shown with the root C. Regardless of what the root of a chord may be, the intervals between the chord members, when arranged in their simplest position, are always the same for any specific type of chord. It is important to keep in mind that the identity and name of the chord are unchanged, no matter in what way the component notes are arranged.

A MAJOR chord consists of the root, plus a note a major 3rd above the root (this note is called the 3rd of the chord) plus a note a perfect 5th above the root, the latter note being called the 5th of the chord.

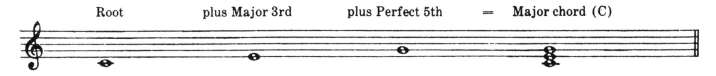

A MINOR chord consists of the root, a minor 3rd, and a perfect 5th.

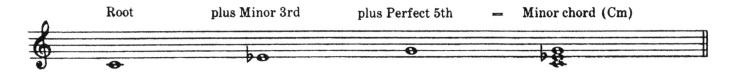

A DOMINANT SEVENTH chord consists of a major chord plus a note a minor 7th above the root.

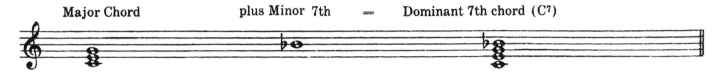

A DIMINISHED SEVENTH chord consists of the root, a minor 3rd, a diminished 5th, and a diminished 7th. When analyzed, this chord proves to be a series of minor 3rds, one on top of the other.

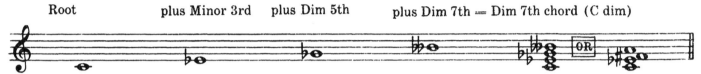

An AUGMENTED FIFTH chord is a major 3rd plus a note an augmented 5th above the root. It can be considered to be two major 3rds, one on top of the other.

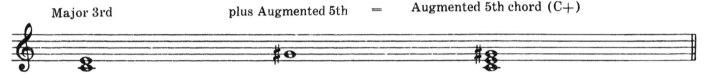

A MINOR SEVENTH chord is a minor chord plus a note a minor 7th above the root.

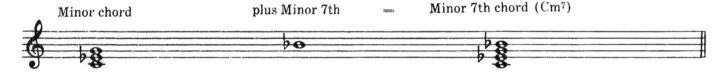

The construction of other chords will be shown as they are introduced.

As played on the guitar, frequently a particular note appears more than once in a chord. Also, it is impossible to use all of the chord notes in the playing of some chords. However, in planning a chord form, an attempt is always made to include the chord notes that give the chord an unmistakable identity.

THIRD SERIES OF CHORDS

For accompanying popular and jazz music in a manner producing the most rhythmic beat, the following procedure is usually used. A straight chord accompaniment is played; no basses are used. The chord played on the 1st count in each measure is sustained for a full count. The chord on the 2nd count is played short by momentarily lifting the left-hand fingers immediately after the chord has been sounded. The chord on the 3rd count is sustained. The chord on the 4th count is played short. Thus, each measure will sound "long-short, long-short."

For this purpose, the most effective chord formations are those producing a sound with depth and body, and in which all six strings may be included in the stroke. To achieve these results, many chord formations are used in which one or two of the strings are muted or deadened. An "X" in a small circle above a string will show where a string is to be muted by touching it lightly with a convenient portion of a conveniently located left-hand finger.

In showing the chords in this series, the top line of the diagram no longer indicates the nut. Instead, the portion of the fingerboard to be used can be determined by the numbers appearing on the right side of the diagram, showing the frets represented.

The specific chord formations shown in this series were selected carefully from the many, many possibilities as being the most practical for the purpose. These are the most satisfactory chord formations for use in playing rhythm guitar in a combo, a dance orchestra, and a stage band.

MAJOR CHORDS

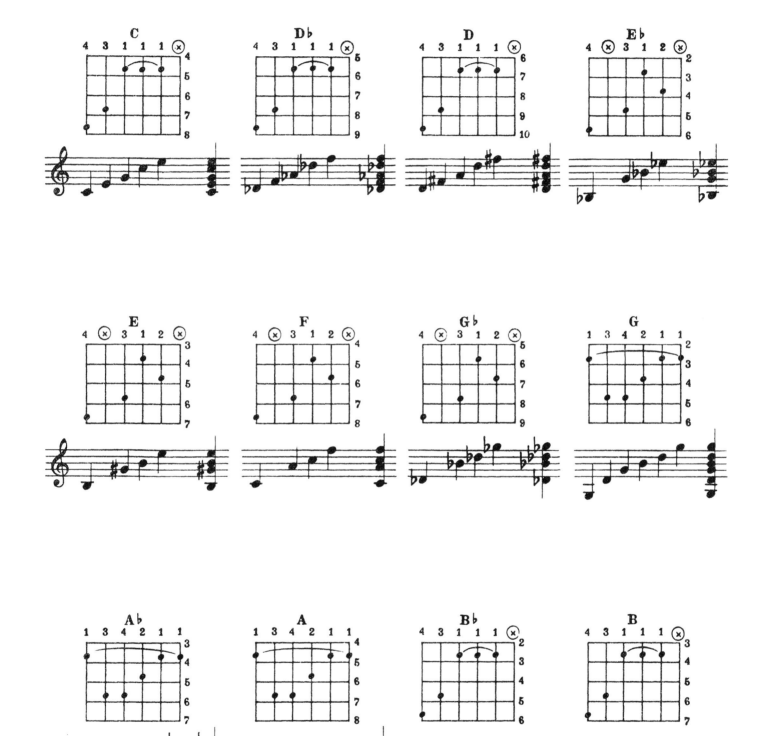

Note: Many of the chord formations shown in this series are useful even higher on the fingerboard than shown. Some of them are useful in positions lower on the fingerboard than shown.

MINOR CHORDS

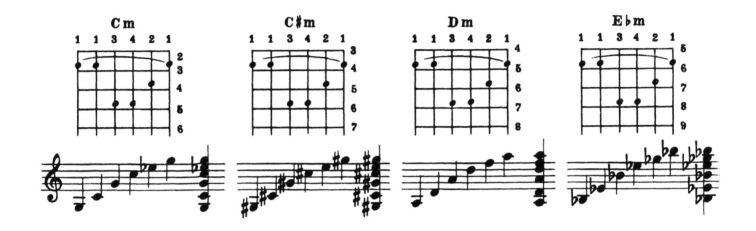

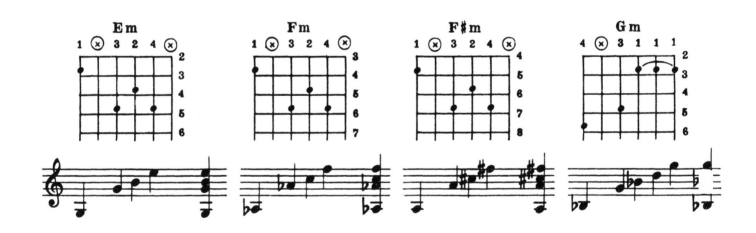

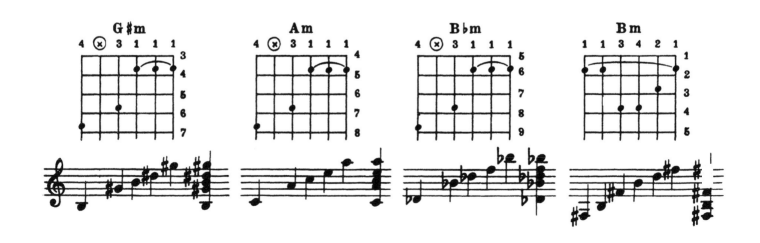

DOMINANT SEVENTH CHORDS

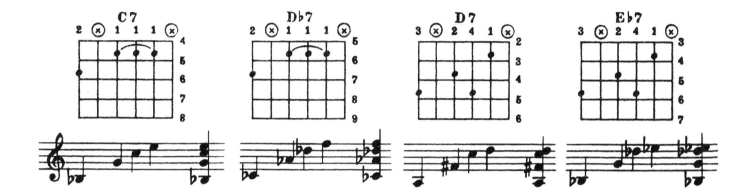

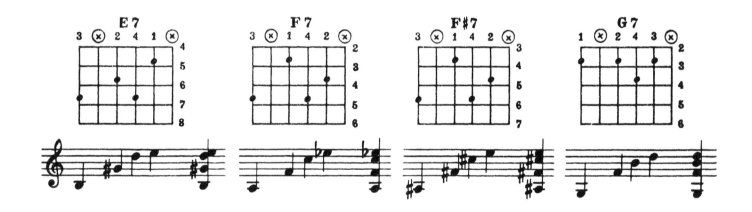

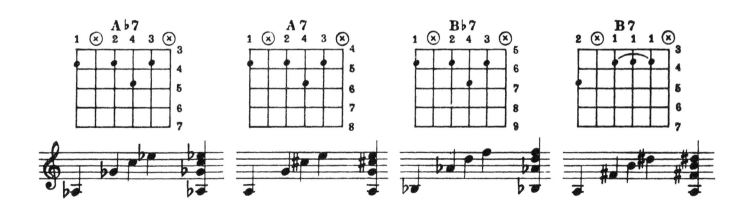

DIMINISHED SEVENTH CHORDS

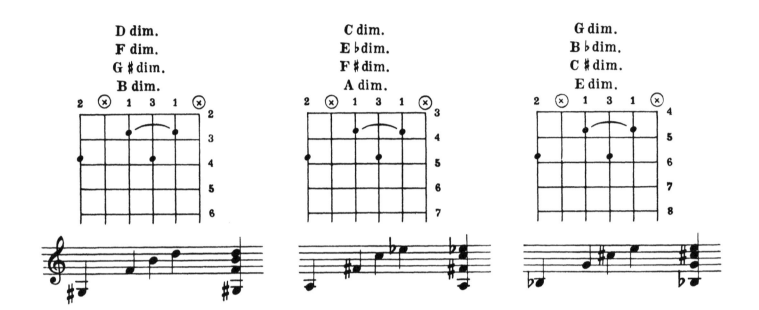

AUGMENTED FIFTH CHORDS

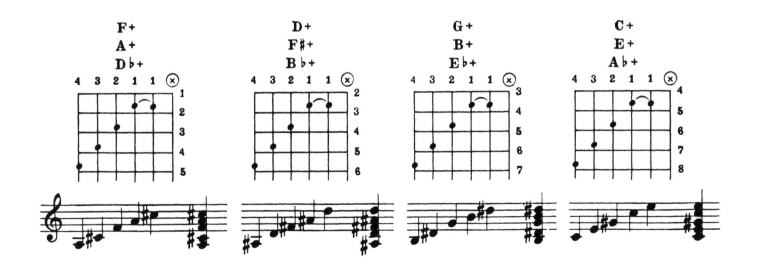

MINOR SEVENTH CHORDS

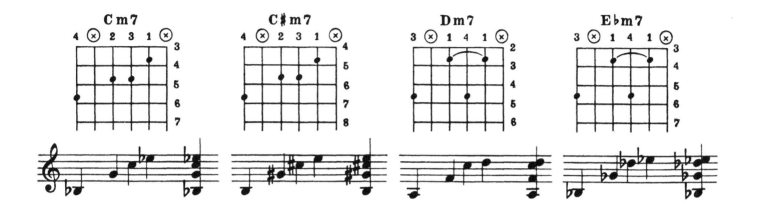

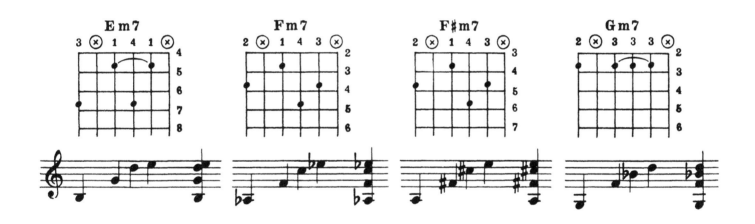

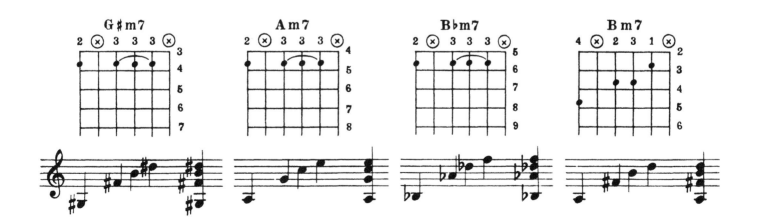

FOURTH SERIES OF CHORDS

This series consists of chords with a structure more complex than those so far shown. Each chord is given in two versions. The first version shown is comparable to chords in the first series; the second is a rhythm type of chord such as those in the third series. Below is an explanation of the construction of the chords in this series.

The major 6th chord (symbol: 6) is a major chord plus a note a major 6th above the root.

The minor 6th chord (symbol: m6) is a minor chord plus a note a major 6th above the root.

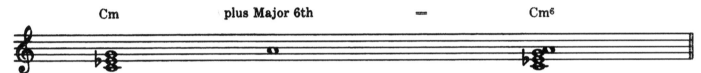

There is a chord called "minor seventh diminished fifth" (symbol: m7-5) not shown in this book. This chord has the same notes as a minor 6th chord whose root is a minor 3rd higher.

Example: Am7-5 = Cm6.

The major 7th chord (symbol: ma7) is a major chord plus a note a major 7th above the root.

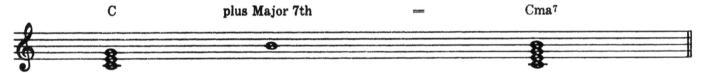

The dominant 7th augmented 5th chord (symbol: 7+5) is a dominant 7th chord with its 5th altered upward a half-step.

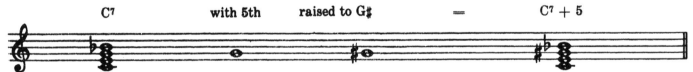

The dominant 7th diminished 5th chord (symbol: 7-5) is a dominant 7th chord with its 5th altered downward a half-step.

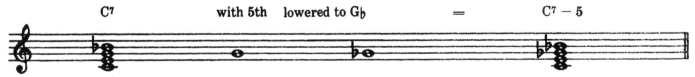

The dominant 9th chord (symbol: 9) is a dominant 7th chord plus a note a major 9th above the root.

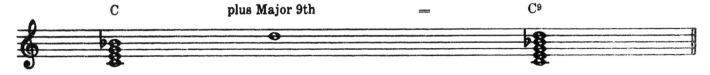

The dominant 9th augmented 5th chord (symbol: 9+5) is a dominant 9th chord with its 5th altered upward a half-step.

The dominant 9th diminished 5th chord (symbol: 9-5) is a dominant 9th chord with its 5th altered downward a half-step.

The dominant 7th minor 9th chord (symbol: 7-9) is a dominant 7th chord plus a note a minor 9th above the root.

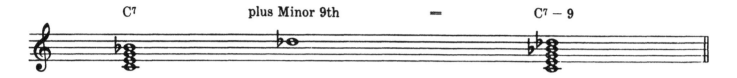

The dominant 11th chord (symbol: 11) is a dominant 9th chord plus a note a perfect 11th above the root. In playing this chord, the 3rd of the chord should never be included.

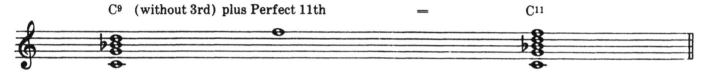

The augmented 11th chord (symbol: 11+) is a dominant 11th chord with its 11th altered upward a half-step. In this chord the 5th is usually left out.

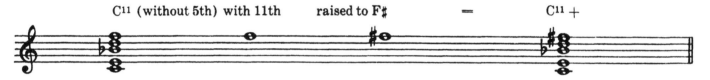

The dominant 13th chord (symbol: 13) is a dominant 9th chord plus a note a major 13th above the root. This chord should never include the 11th.

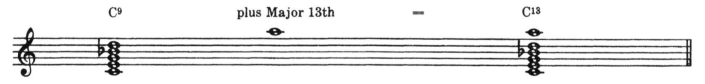

The dominant 13th minor 9th chord (symbol: 13-9) is a dominant 13th chord with its 9th altered downward a half-step.

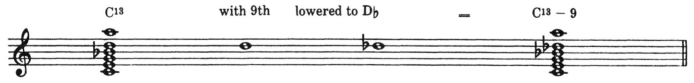

The major 6th add 9th chord (symbol: $\frac{9}{6}$ or 6 add 9) is a major 6th chord plus a note a major 9th above the root.

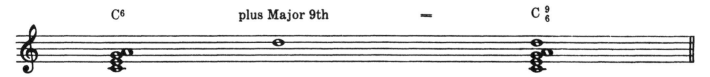

MAJOR SIXTH CHORDS

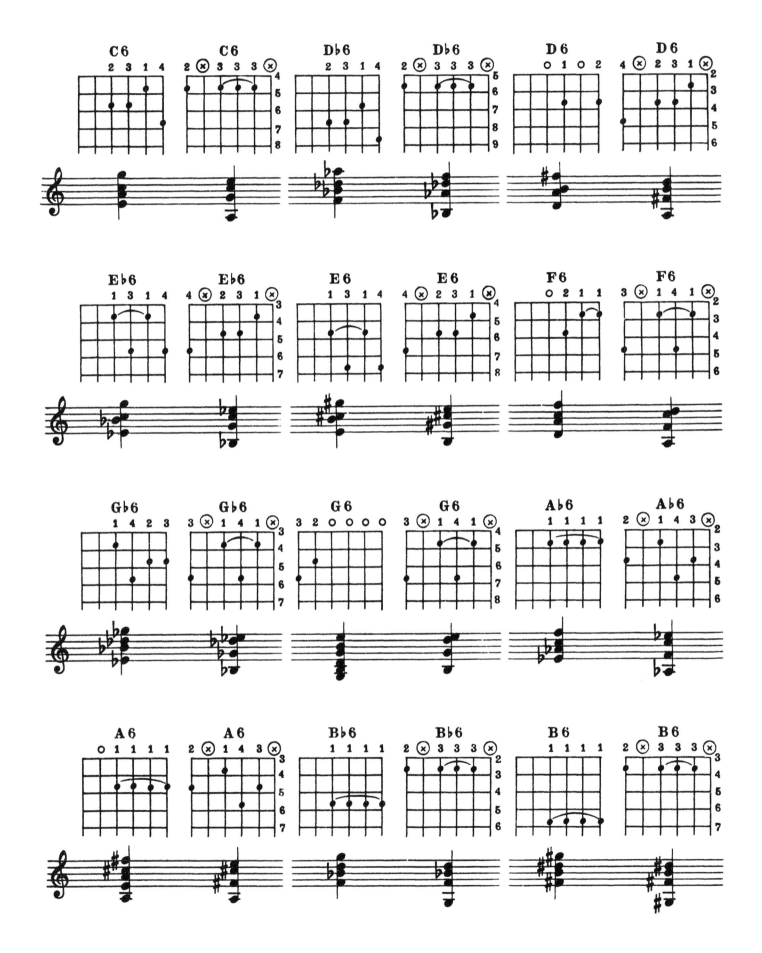

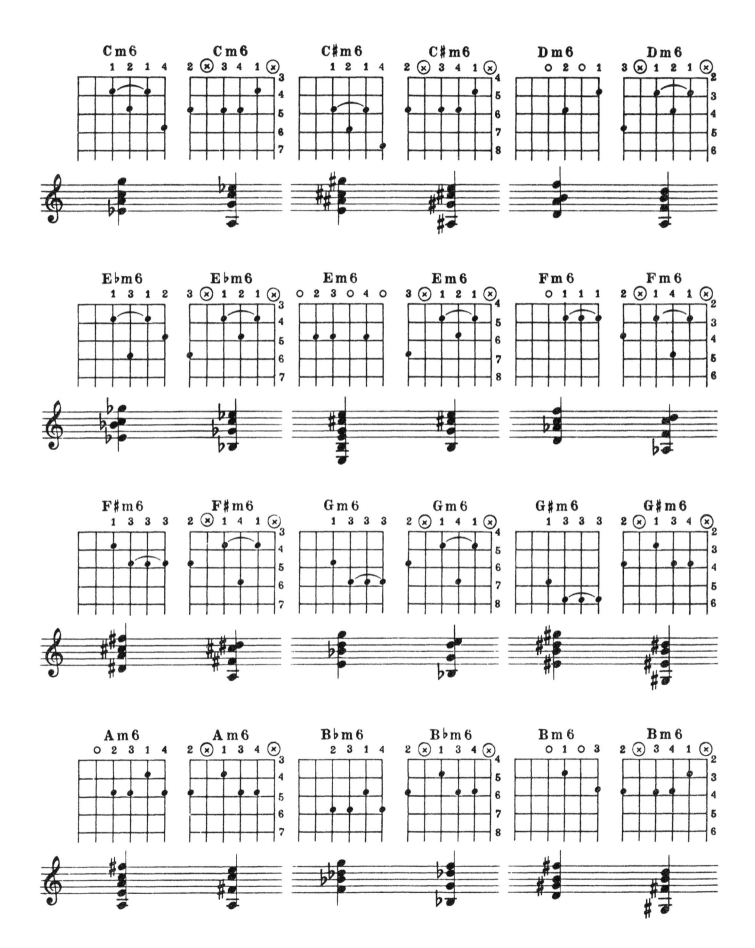

MINOR SIXTH CHORDS

MAJOR SEVENTH CHORDS

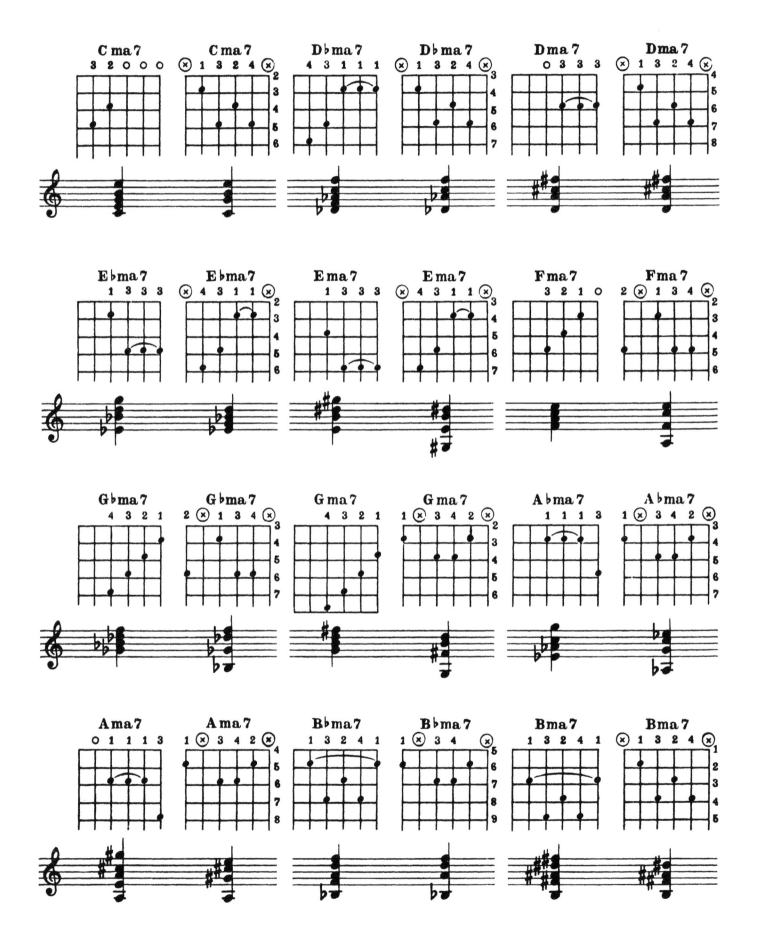

DOMINANT SEVENTH AUGMENTED FIFTH CHORDS

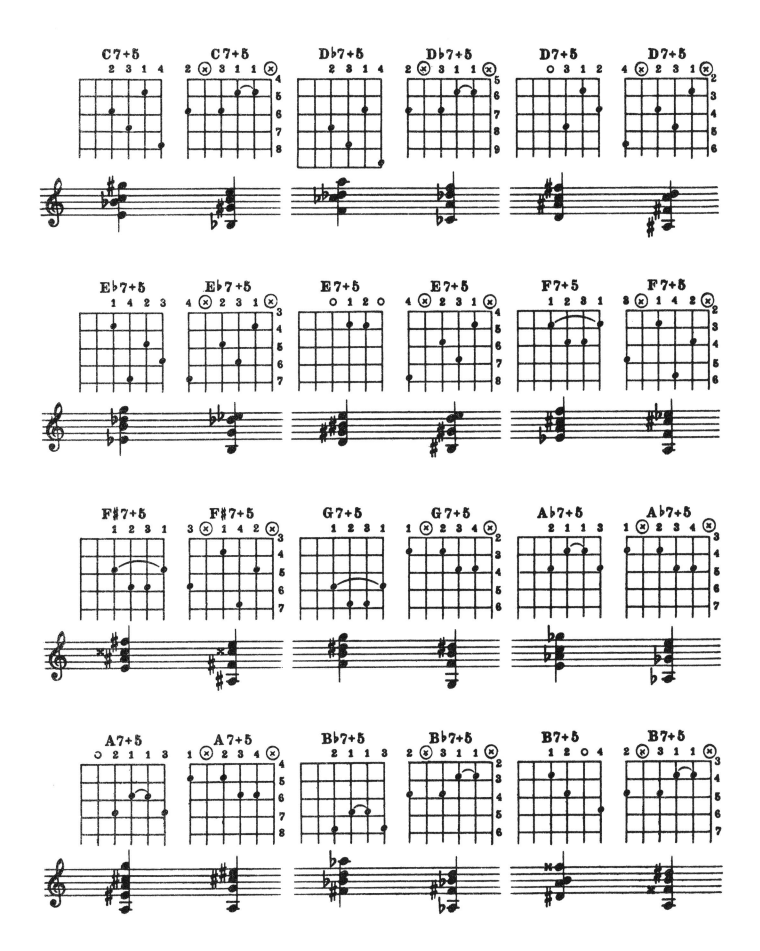

DOMINANT SEVENTH DIMINISHED FIFTH CHORDS

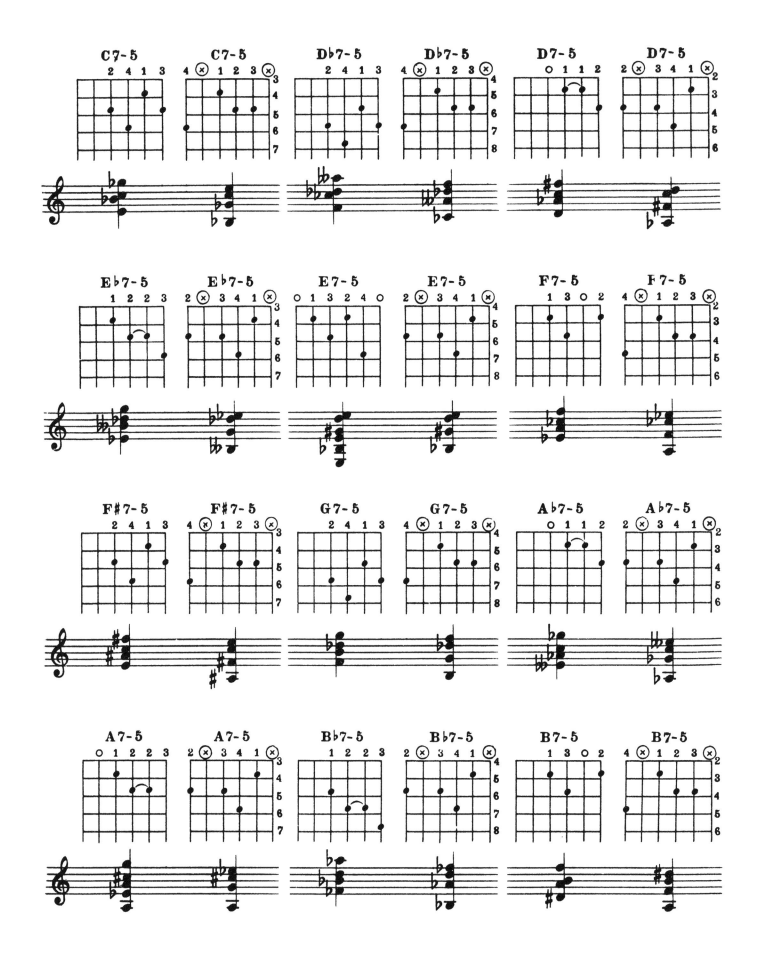

DOMINANT NINTH CHORDS

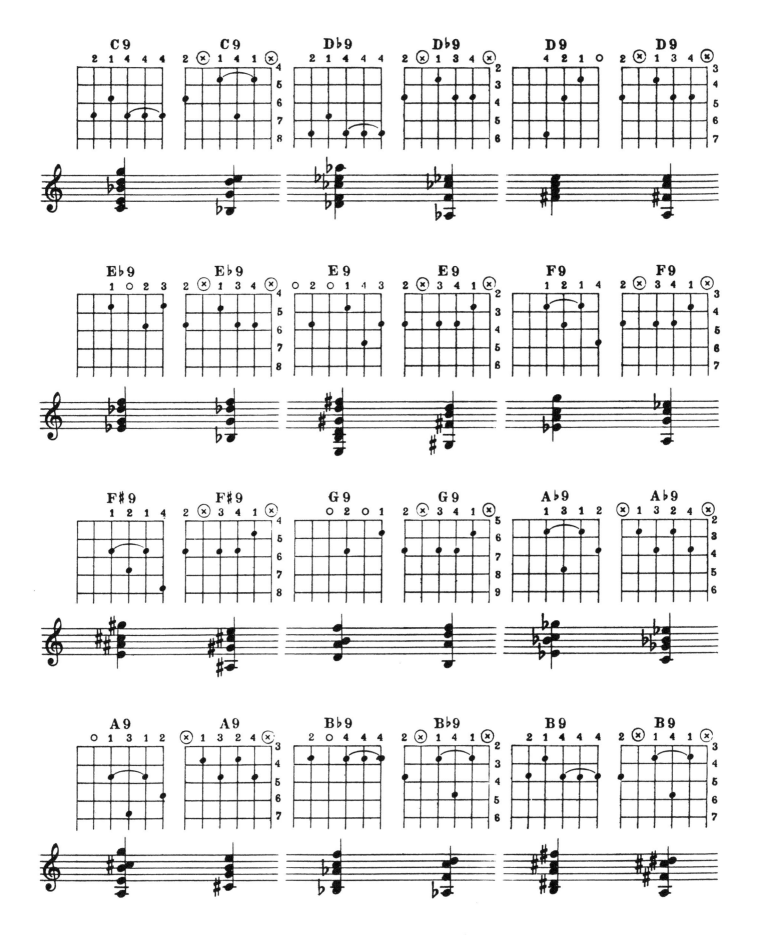

DOMINANT NINTH AUGMENTED FIFTH CHORDS

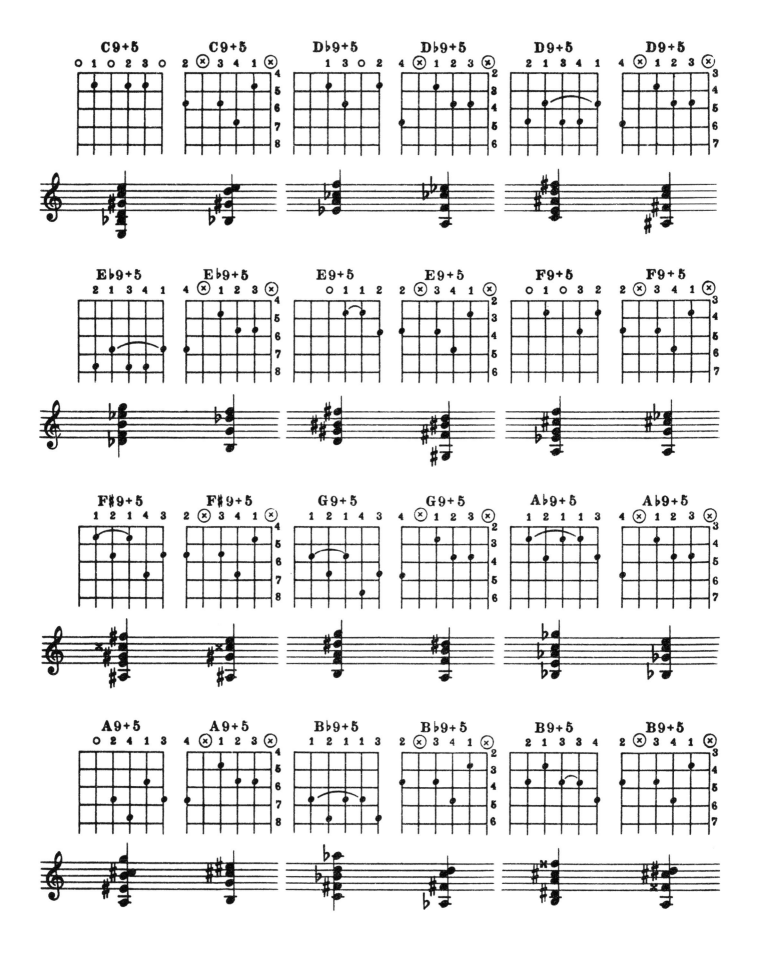

DOMINANT NINTH DIMINISHED FIFTH CHORDS

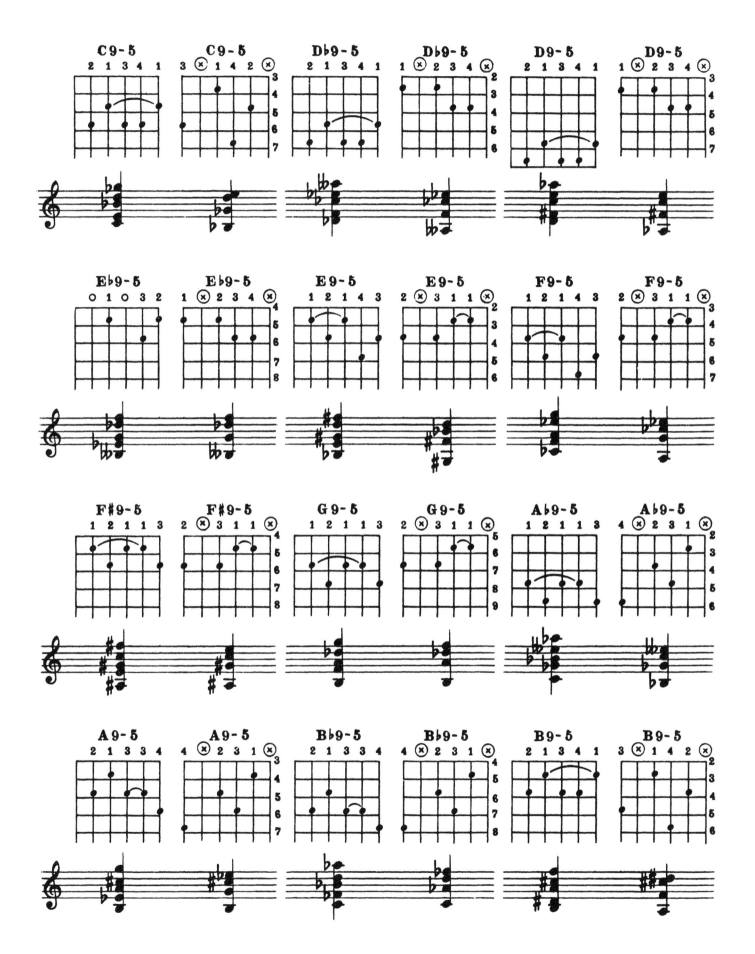

DOMINANT SEVENTH MINOR NINTH CHORDS

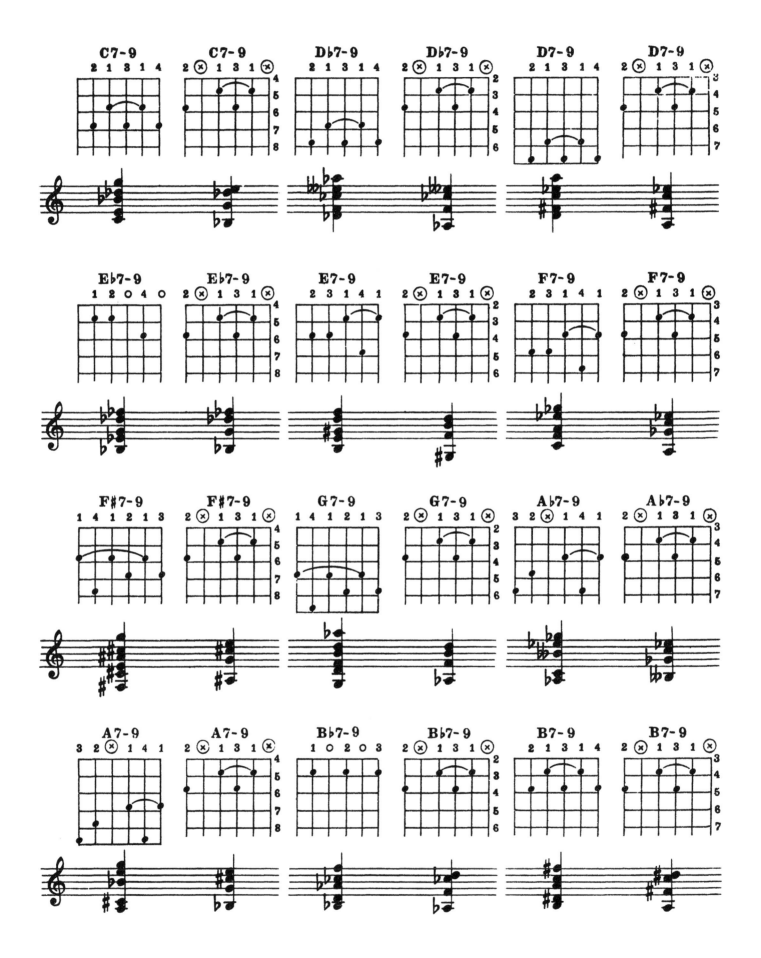

DOMINANT ELEVENTH CHORDS

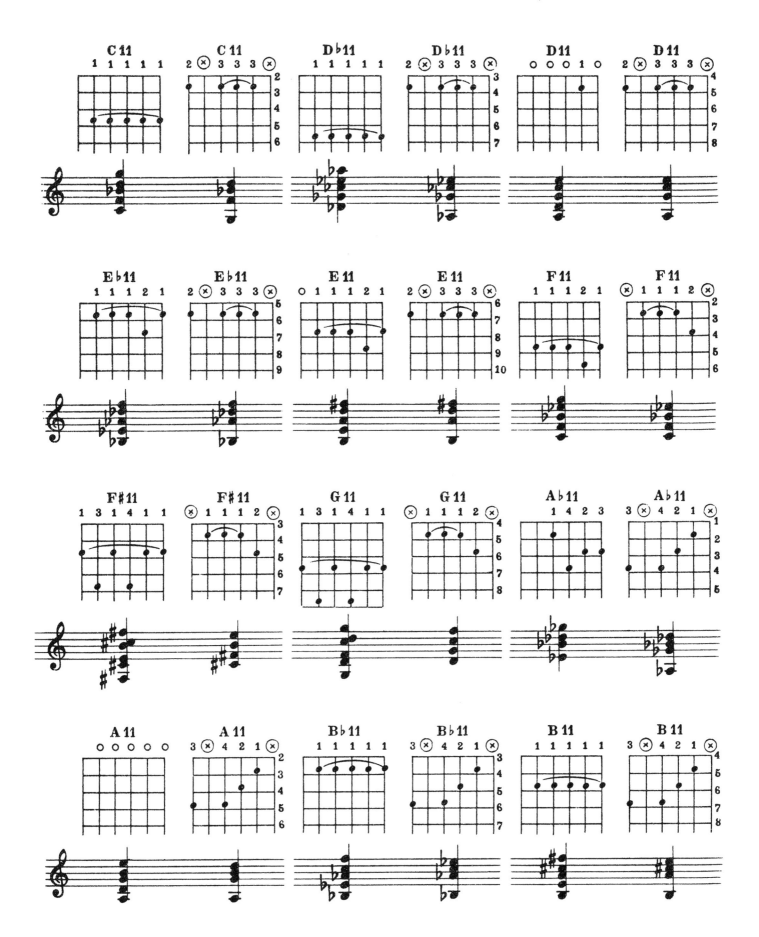

AUGMENTED ELEVENTH CHORDS

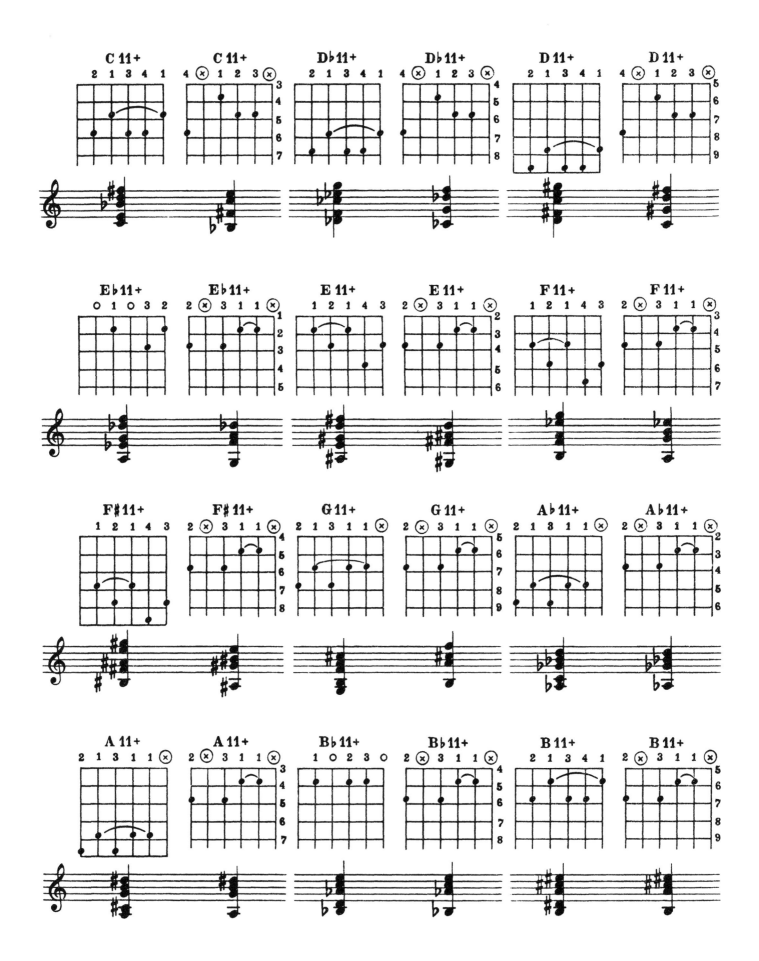

DOMINANT THIRTEENTH CHORDS

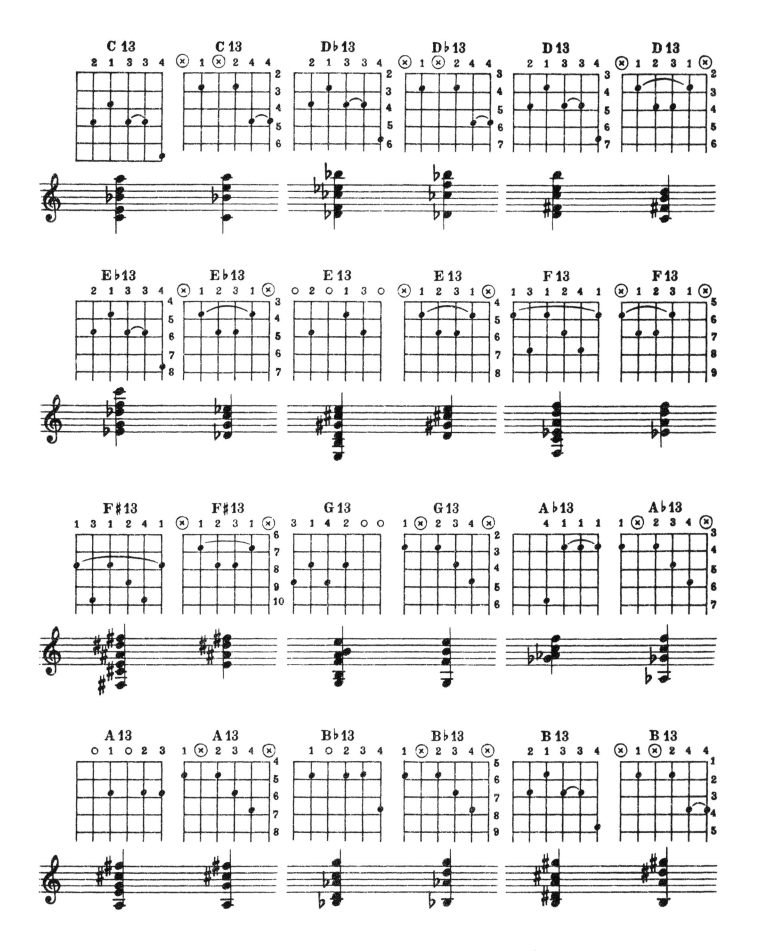

DOMINANT THIRTEENTH MINOR NINTH CHORDS

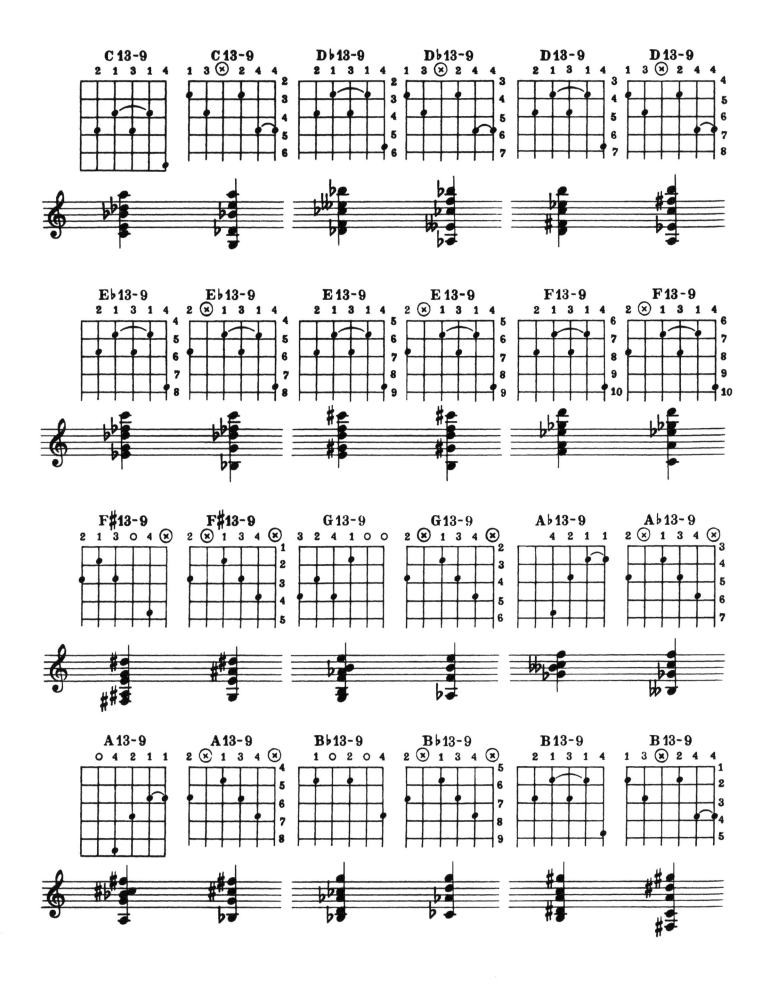

MAJOR SIXTH ADD NINTH CHORDS

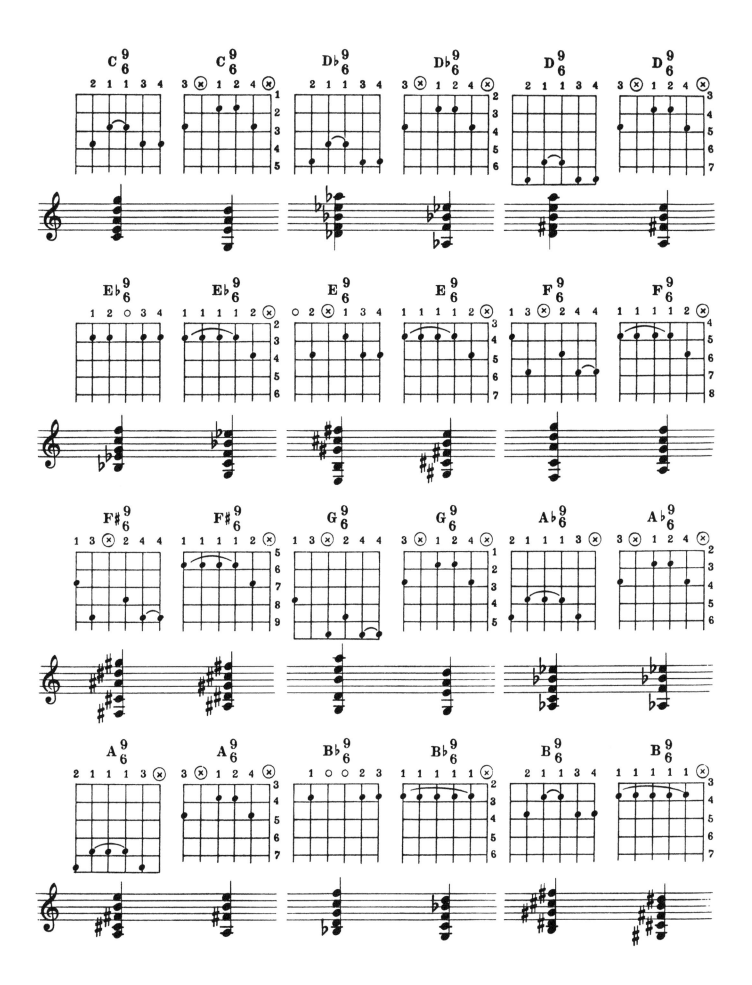

Chord Progressions

PART I - ELEMENTARY

These are basic chord progressions found in folk songs and in songs with simple harmonic development. Practicing these will open for early grade students a large repertoire of standard tunes. The diagrams are optional. You may substitute another form of the chord from the wide choice in this book. In the simplest form of tri-chord progression, the first of the two 7th chords may be omitted.

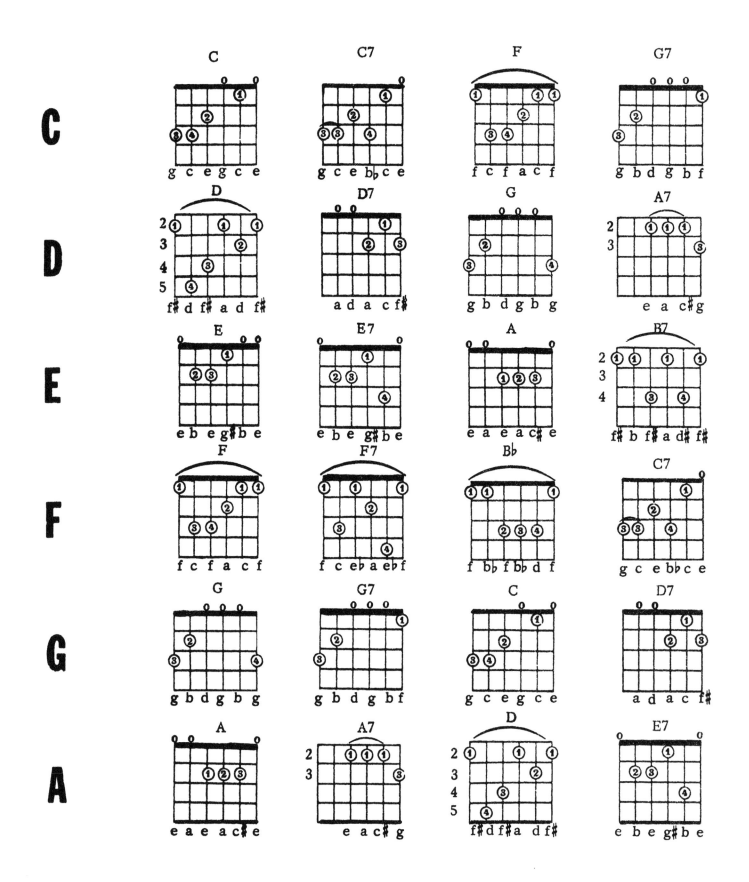

Chord Progressions

PART II - 8-CHORD PROGRESSIONS

There is no set pattern for chord progressions, because they vary with the melodic concept. It is suggested that you practice these progressions which, with some variations, are found very frequently. Practice the progressions listed below, with position indicated or selected. This will make you feel "at home" as you encounter the progressions in playing.

In "rock progressions", the guitarist will often follow major chords with 7th's and 6th's - to expand the sound. Major 7th chords are frequently used as a "go between" from major chords to 7th chords.

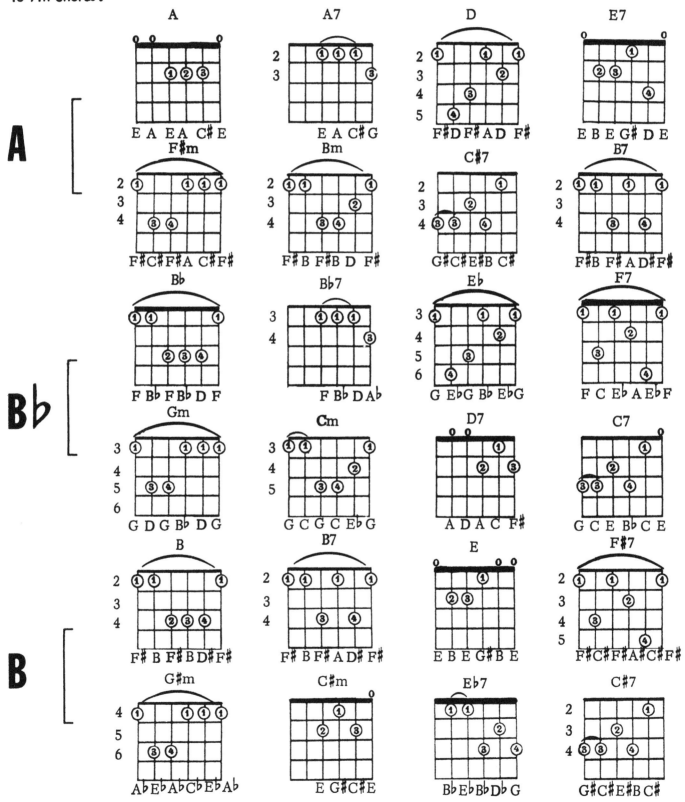

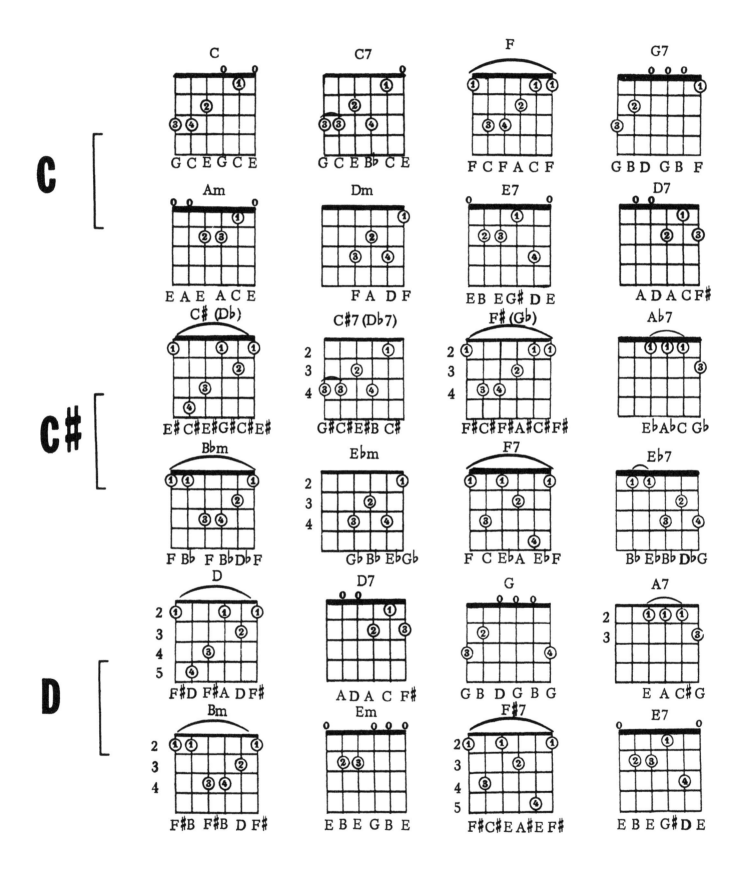

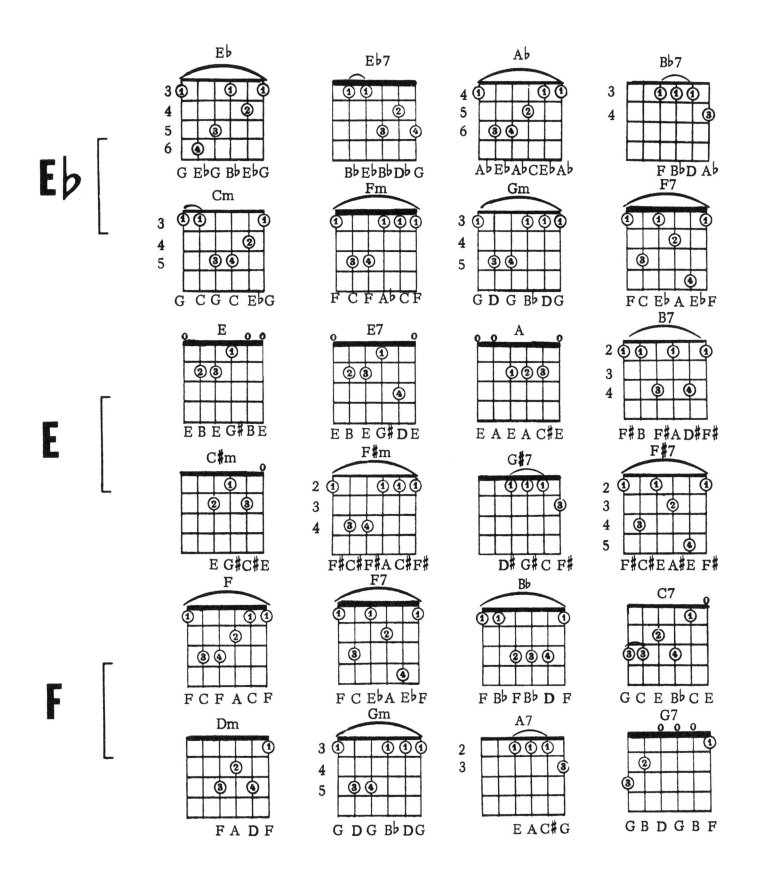

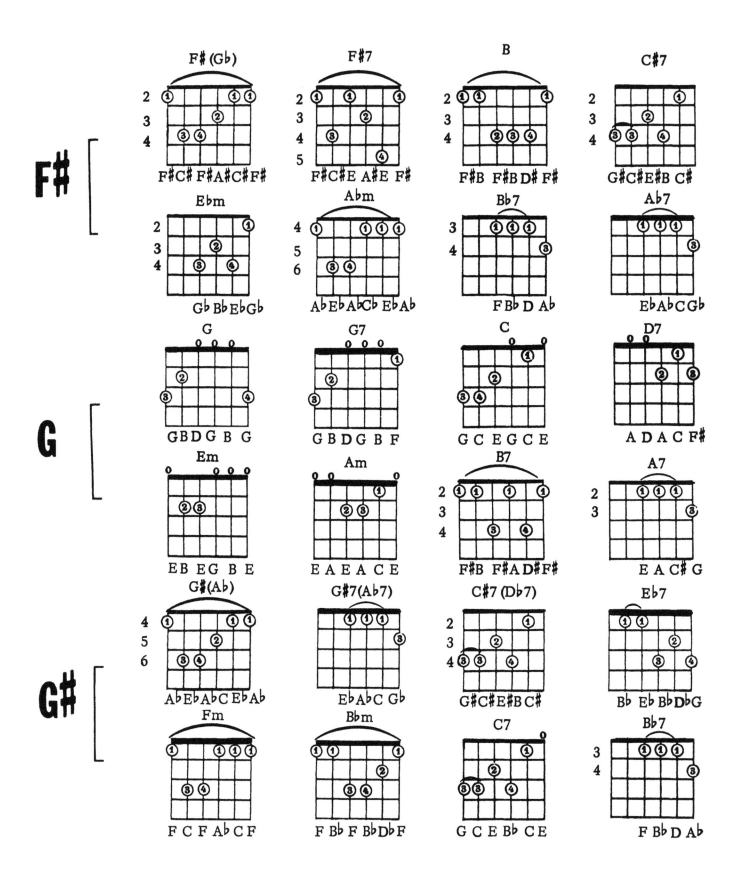

Chord Progressions

Part III – 4-CHORD PROGRESSIONS IN MINOR KEYS

A review of these common progressions in minor keys should be made and put into practical operation by trying out these chords in the minor key songs appearing in this book. Here again the diagrams may be played as shown or as selected from other diagrams in specific sections.

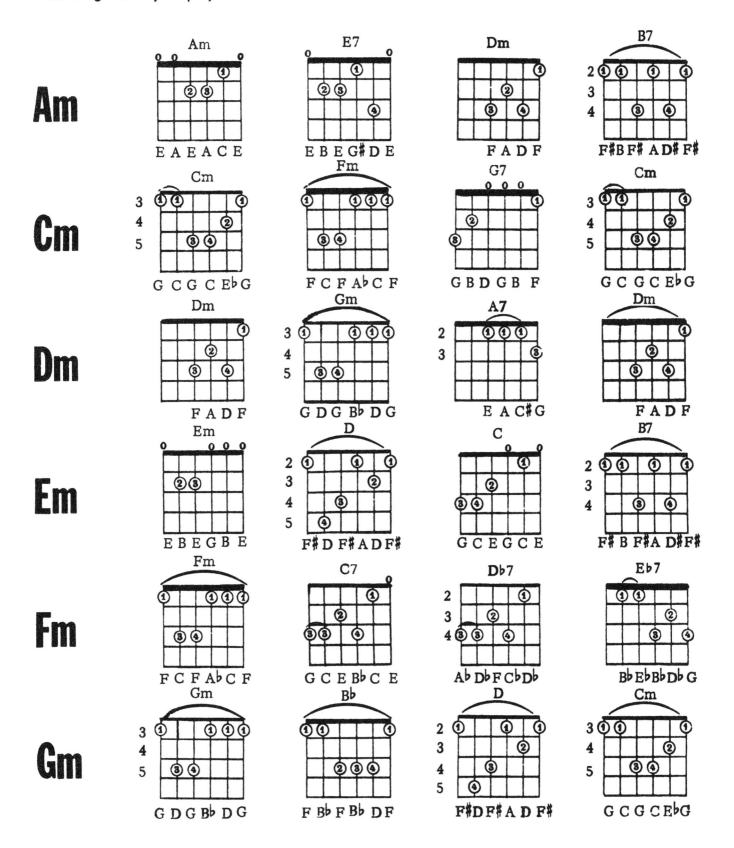

BASIC GUITAR CHORDS

THE FOLLOWING CHORDS ARE SHOWN IN THE BASIC FORMS FAVORED FOR "PICKING AND STRUMMING" AND FOR SIMPLE ACCOMPANIMENT TO POPULAR SONGS.

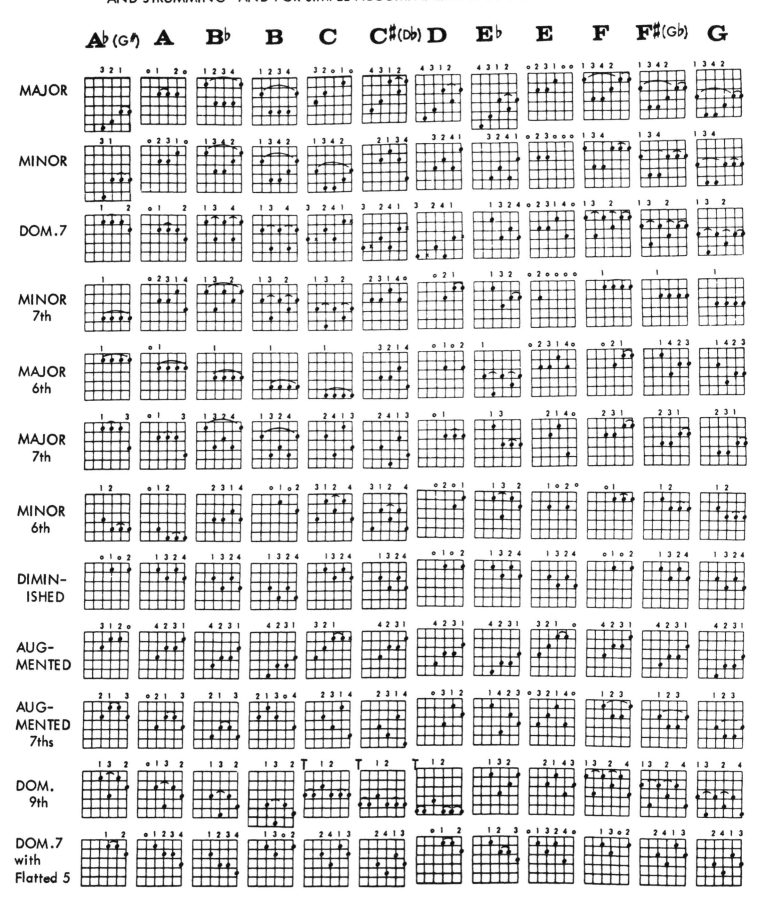

SCALES

SECTION II

THE STUDY OF SCALES IS AN IMPORTANT FACTOR IN MASTERING THE GUITAR. IN PUTTING THIS BOOK TOGETHER WE CAME UP WITH AN EFFECTIVE WAY TO HELP YOU ACHIEVE THIS PHASE OF STUDY.

WE FEEL THAT THIS MATERIAL IS GOOD GROUND WORK, AND A BIG STEP FORWARD ON BECOMING A FINE GUITARIST.

THE PUBLISHER.

*****CONTENTS*****

Scale of C Major

two sixteenth and eighth notes

eighth, quarter and eighth notes

triplets

eighth and two sixteenth notes

Scale of A Minor, Melodic Form

(Relative to C Major)

Scale of G Major

Scale of E Minor, Melodic Form
(Relative to G Major)

Scale of D Major

Scale of B Minor, Melodic Form
(Relative to D Major)

Scale of A Major

Scale of F♯ Minor, Melodic Form

(Relative to A Major)

Scale of E Major

Scale of C# Minor, Melodic Form

(Relative to E Major)

Scale of F Major

Scale of D Minor, Melodic Form
(Relative to F Major)

Scale of B♭ Major

Scale of G Minor, Melodic Form

(Relative to B♭ Major)

Scale of E♭ Major

Scale of C Minor, Melodic Form
(Relative to E♭ Major)

Scale of A♭ Major

Scale of F Minor, Melodic Form
(Relative to A♭ Major)

Other Suggested Rhythms

COMPOUND TIME

D Major Scale

(2nd position)

A♭ Major Scale

(1st position)

C 7th Run

A 7th Run

G 7th Run

The above Runs should be practiced
chromatically to insure a thorough
knowledge of these scales in all keys.

Accompaniment Styles

The above Styles should be practiced
chromatically to insure knowledge of all keys.

All these styles are very effective
for vocal background.

INDEX TO FRETS AND STRINGS

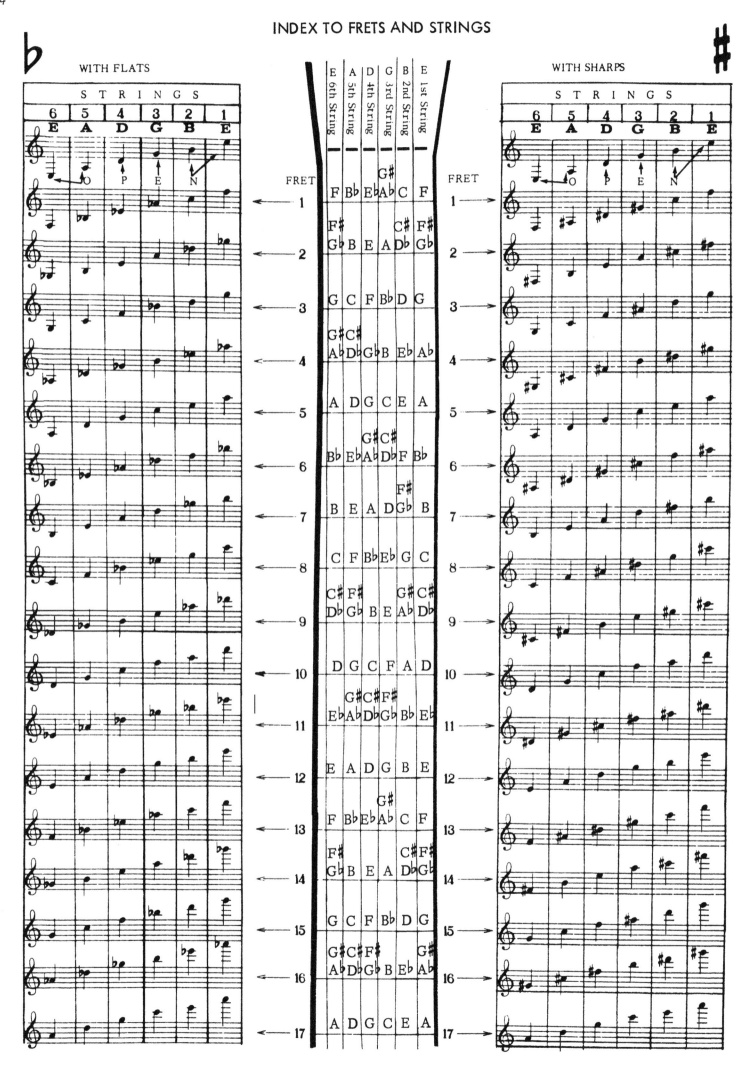

	E 6th String	A 5th String	D 4th String	G 3rd String	B 2nd String	E 1st String
FRET				G#		
1	F	B♭	E♭	A♭	C	F
2	F# G♭	B	E	A	C# D♭	F# G♭
3	G	C	F	B♭	D	G
4	G# A♭	C# D♭	G♭	B	E♭	A♭
5	A	D	G	C	E	A
6	B♭	E♭	G# A♭	C# D♭	F	B♭
7	B	E	A	D	F# G♭	B
8	C	F	B♭	E♭	G	C
9	C# D♭	F# G♭	B	E	G# A♭	C# D♭
10	D	G	C	F	A	D
11	E♭	G# A♭	C# D♭	G♭	B♭	E♭
12	E	A	D	G	B	E
13	F	B♭	E♭	G# A♭	C	F
14	F# G♭	B	E	A	C# D♭	F# G♭
15	G	C	F	B♭	D	G
16	G# A♭	C# D♭	G♭ F#	B	E♭	G# A♭
17	A	D	G	C	E	A

BLANK CHORD FRAMES

BLANK CHORD FRAMES

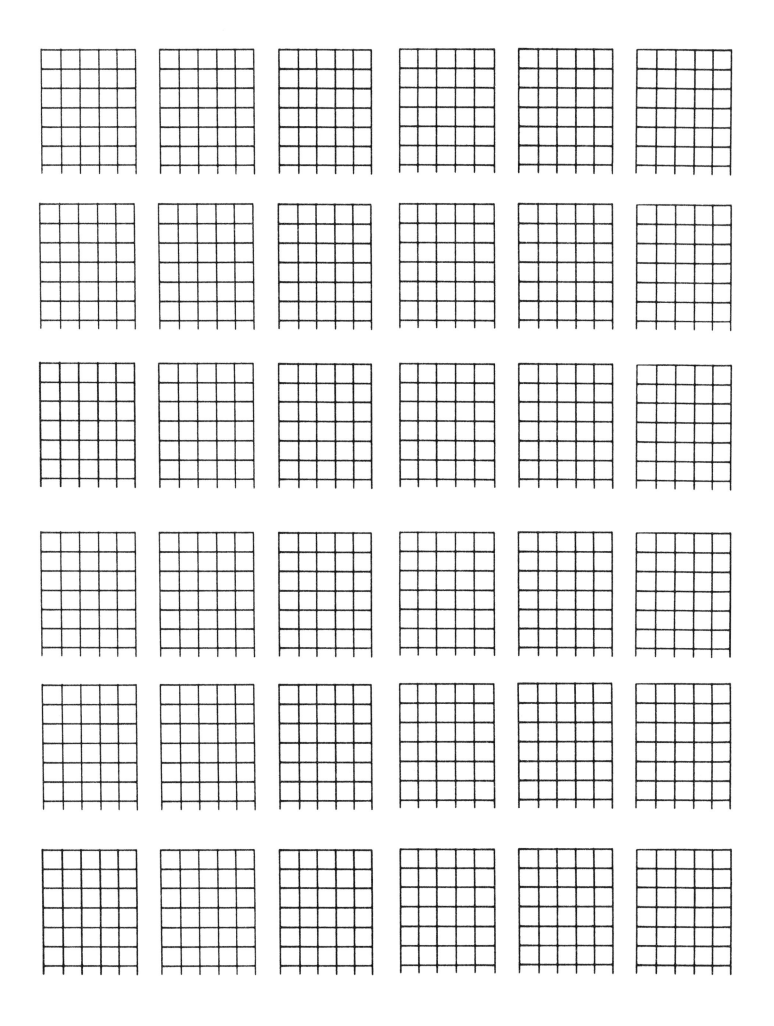

BLANK CHORD FRAMES

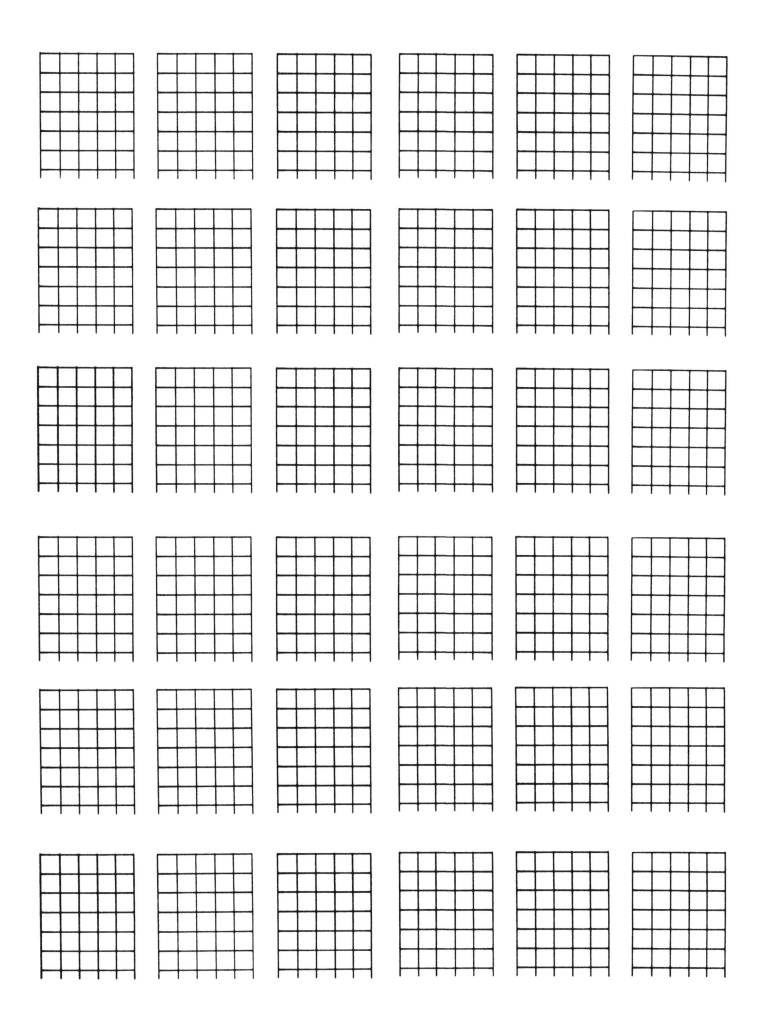

BLANK CHORD FRAMES

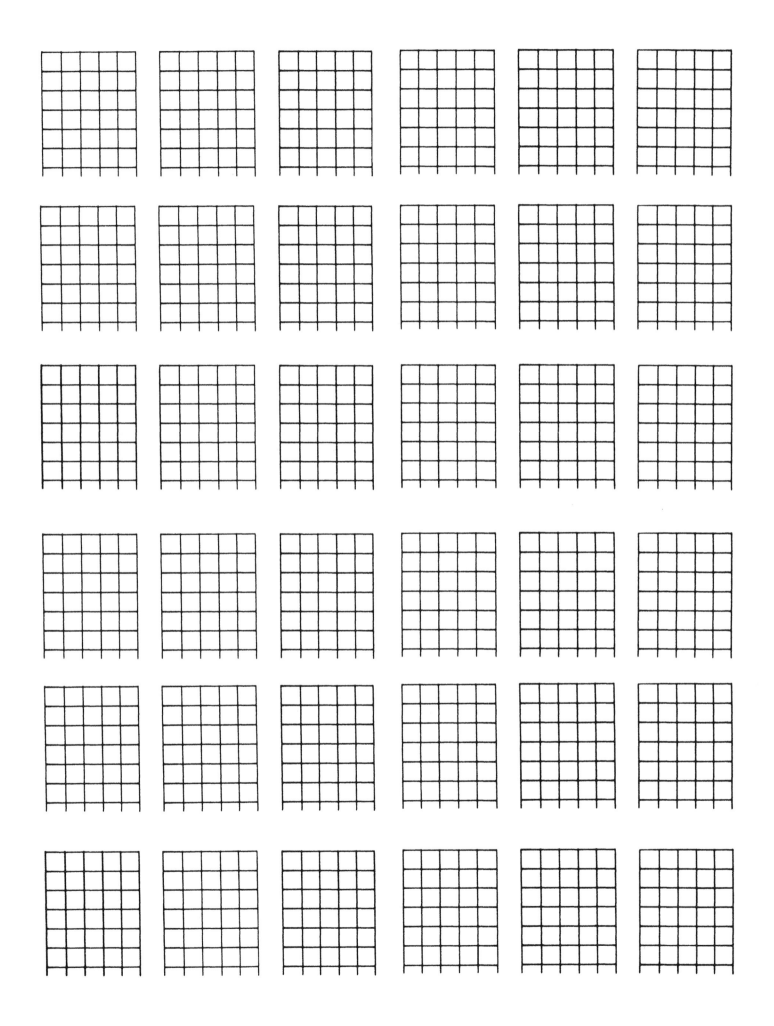

BLANK CHORD FRAMES

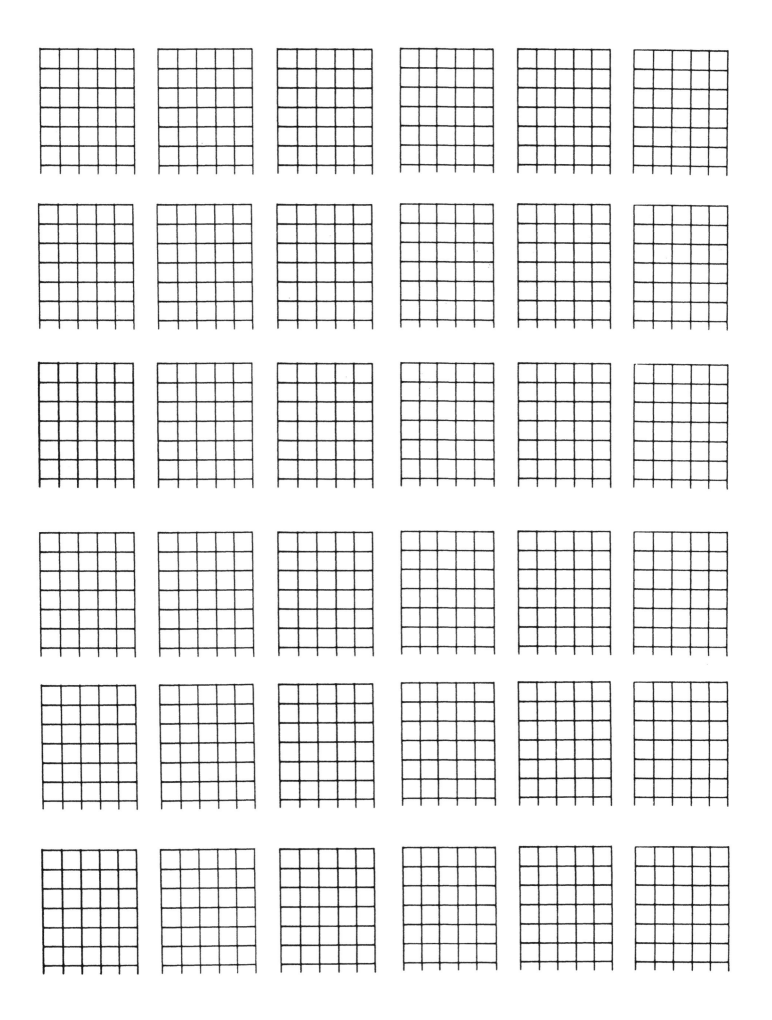

BLANK CHORD FRAMES

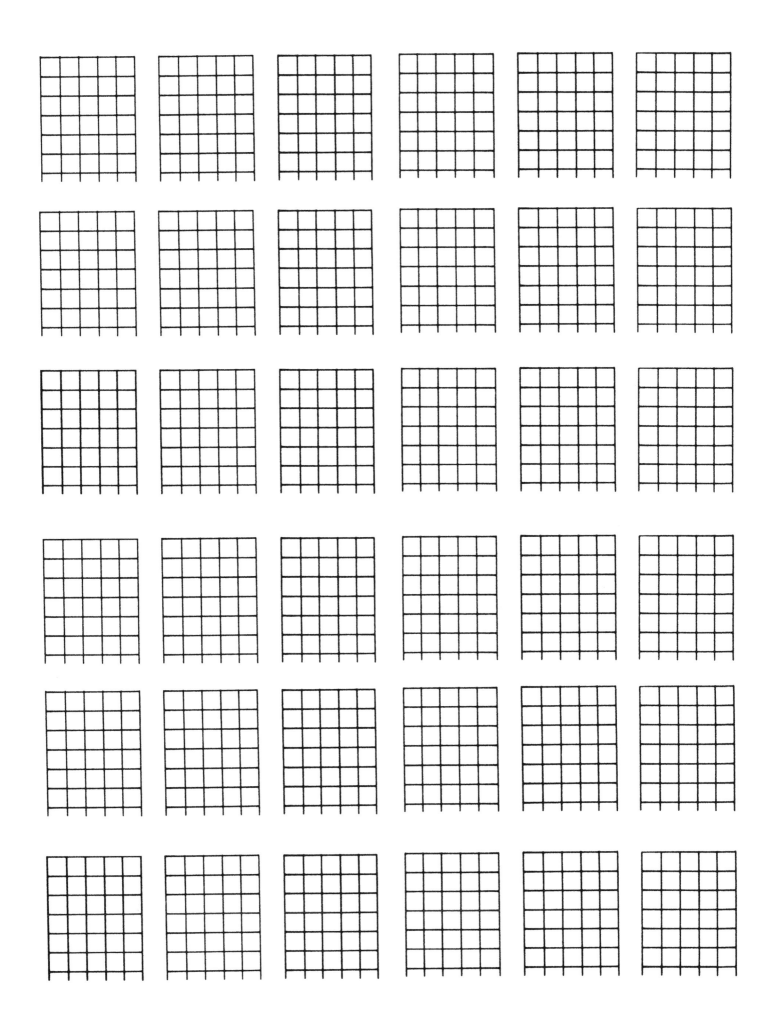

BLANK CHORD FRAMES

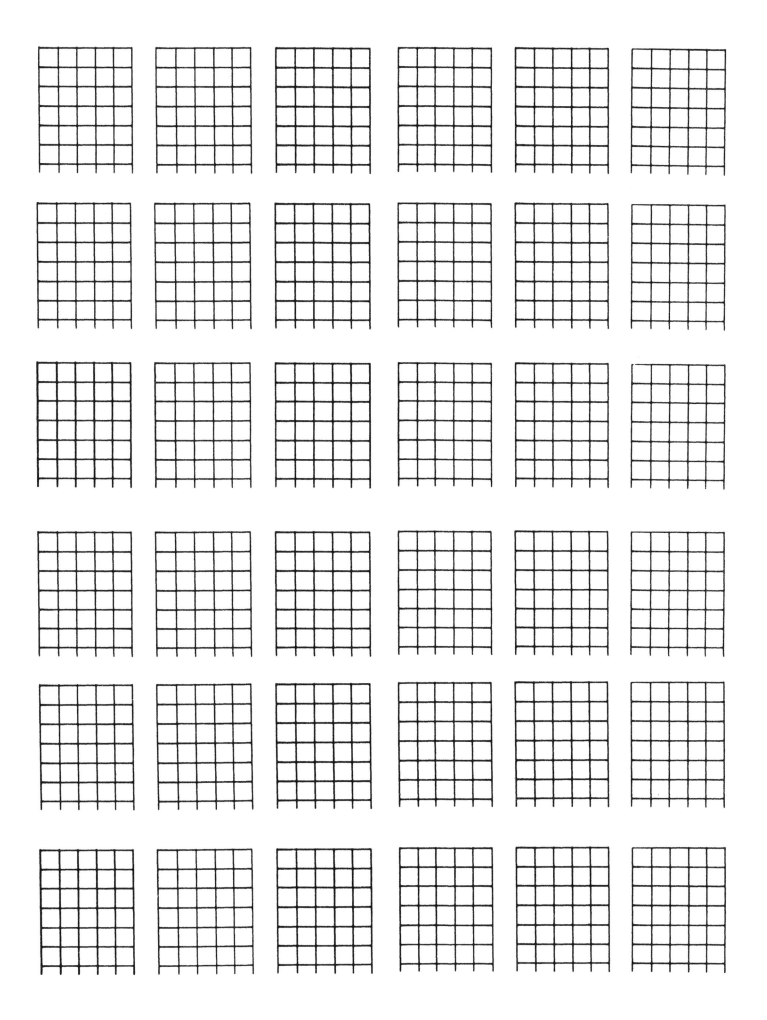

BLANK CHORD FRAMES

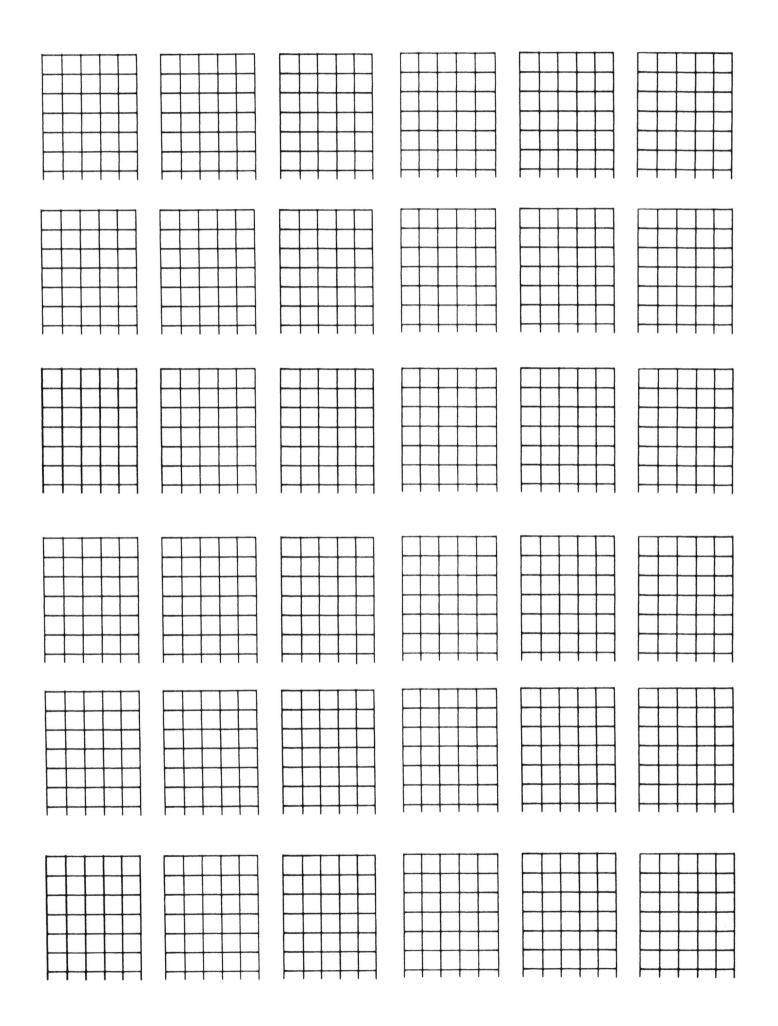

BLANK CHORD FRAMES

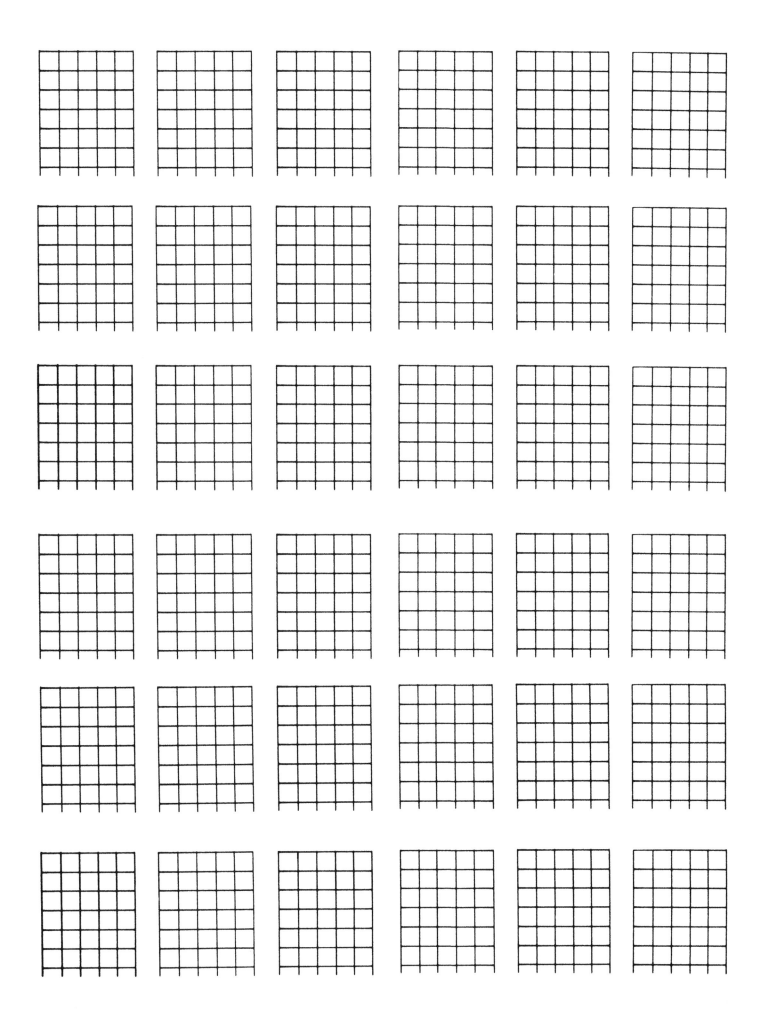

BLANK CHORD FRAMES

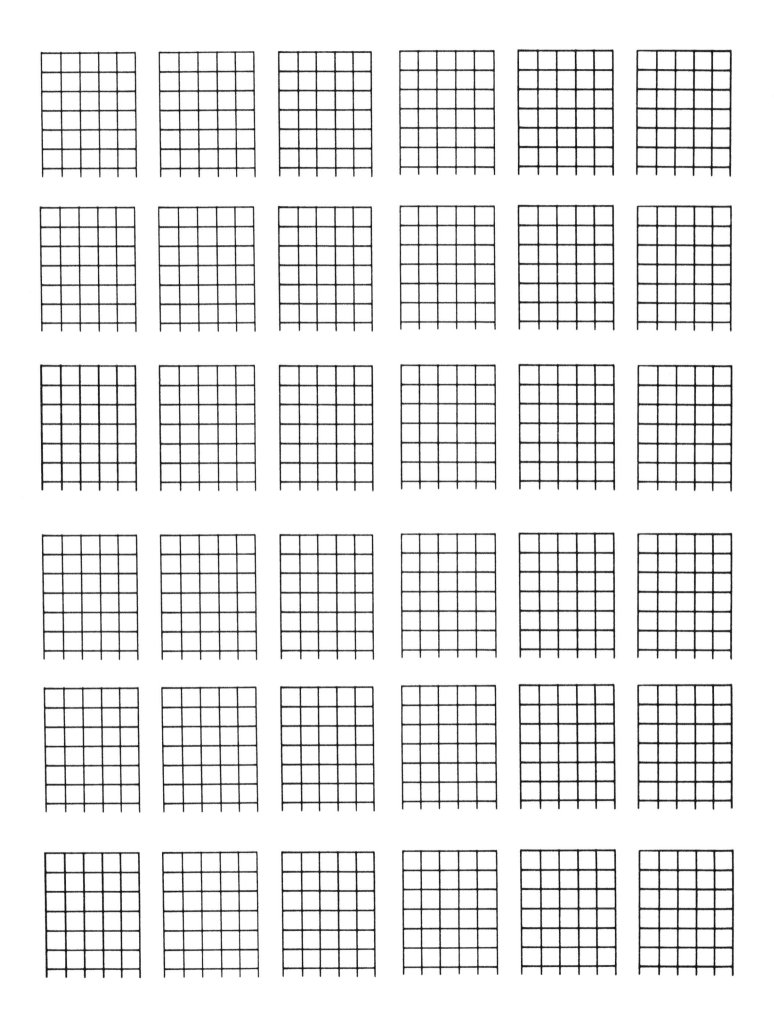

BLANK CHORD FRAMES

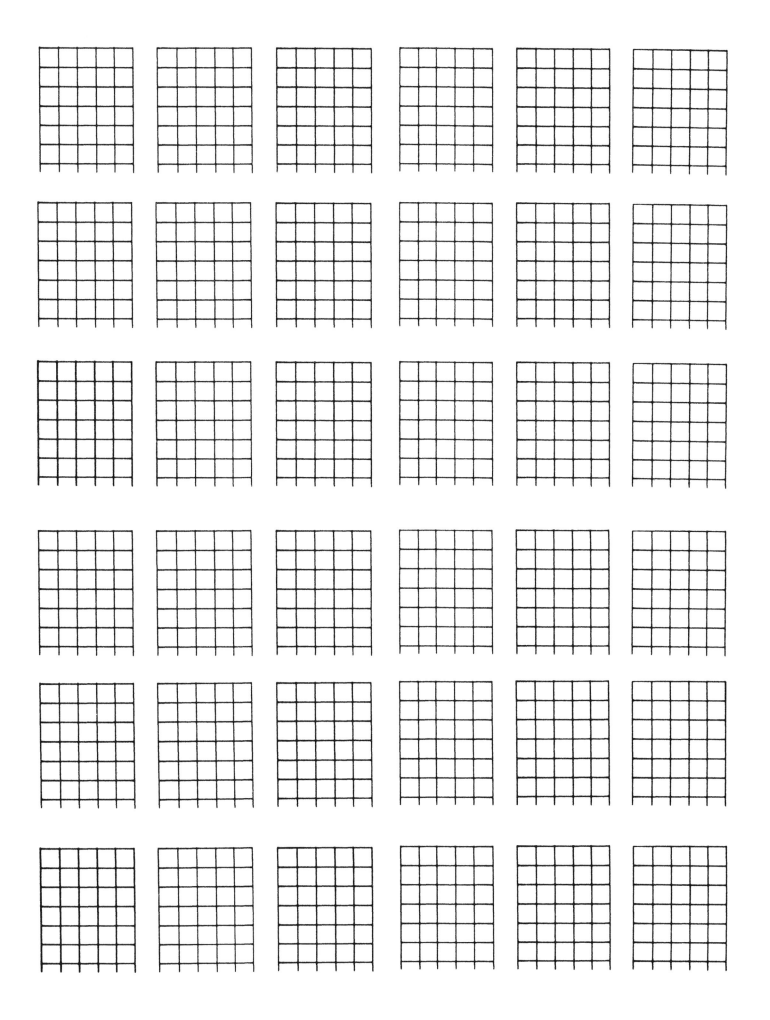

BLANK CHORD FRAMES

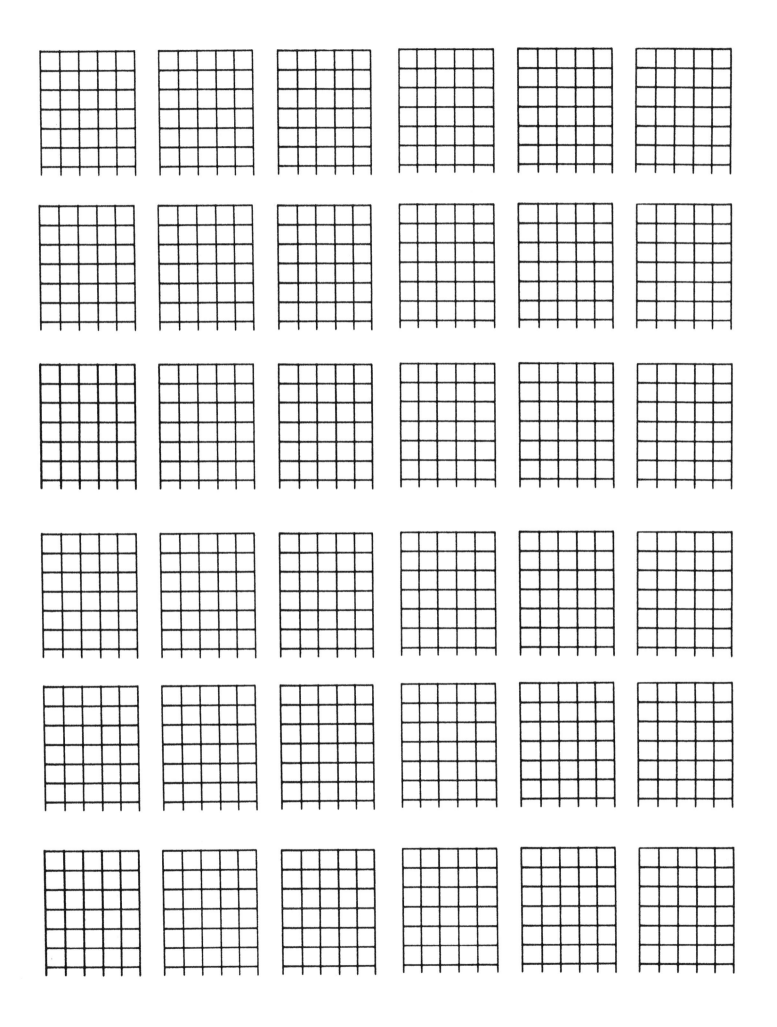